Wake Up & Win
How to Reach Your Goals and Live the Life of Your Dreams

Jermain Miller

With Foreword by Les Brown

Wake Up & Win: How to Reach Your Goals and Live the Life of Your Dreams

DEDICATION

To my grandmother Mildred Gilbert.
If I could make you proud one more time
I pray this book would be the way.
You were my first motivation to live my dreams,
and you still are to this day!
R.I.P. (3/12/1929-5/8/1999)

Love, Jerm

ACKNOWLEDGMENTS

Thank you to my mother and my dad. Without you, I wouldn't be here! To my wife, Michaiah, who showed me what forgiveness and dedication looks like in the manifested world, thank you for believing in me when I had nothing. To my sons Jermain, Jadon, and Johnny and my daughters Trinity and Gabby, thank you for continuing to be my motivation to leave this world better for you. I love you all. To my brother Clayton, I love you.

To my family at the Big House, Thank you for your faith and belief in me.

To my spiritual dad Les Brown, who believed in me and motivated me when I was completely lost and had enough faith in me to take me under his wing; to my editor, Chanel Polk, who didn't see just words on a page, she saw a world changed with this book; to all of my friends whom I call brothers and sisters; to everyone who I had a chance to meet and who was an inspiration to me by saying that I was an inspiration to them, thank you.

To the people I haven't met yet or may never meet in person, I pray this book inspires you to be the greatest version of yourself! Thank you for believing in me!

Thank you, God, for giving me one more day every day to live my dreams so I can impact and empower others to live theirs!

Table of Contents

Foreword

I met Jermain for the first time a few years ago. He was one of the founding members of The Les Brown Institute. I knew from the moment he opened his mouth, he was a force to be reckoned with. Over the years, Jermain has become one of my spiritual sons, and we share similar life stories and like passions. Jermain has been through the fire, and he's come out the wiser for it. His passion to help people get from where they are to where they want to be is unmatched. From his humble beginnings of being raised in a single-parent household, to wanting to buy his grandmother a home and then losing her to cancer. Dropping out of college, from marriage to divorce, to incarceration, homelessness and rock-bottom, sleeping in his office and losing it all to a multi-million dollar producing company... He knows a thing or two about waking up and winning.

In this book, you will learn the secrets to defining what you want and discover how to obtain positive inner conversations with yourself to take the right action steps to achieve your greatness. Jermain shows you how to be a winner, because winners know who they are and what they want.

Individuals who have not yet discovered the keys to greatness will be able to unlock some new opportunities and new experiences for themselves. This book is also for the people who know they are winners, but are out of alignment, out of sync and just need some tweaking, coaching and some adjustments here and there.

So, if you are looking to win in life and are tired of losing, tired of the hard times, setbacks and the struggles, this book is your guide. If you are tired of feeling hopeless and lost, this is an absolute must read. Put yourself to the test and test yourself. In order to do that, you have to believe you can Win!

This is your life. What do you want to achieve while you are here? In order to discover the greatness within, you have to wake up and say to yourself, "I still have an opportunity. As long as I can look up, I can get up! But I have to be open to the possibilities and Wake up and Win."

Les Brown

Introduction

remember being twenty-five years old and waking up on the floor in a basement. I had only ninety-three cents in my bank account. I was at a very deep dark point in my life. A few years prior, I had lost my grandmother and grandfather to cancer. My grandmother had an incredible impact on me growing up and was pretty much my first motivation. Growing up in the 80s and 90s, I had promised her that I would buy her a home and move her out of the drug-infested streets of Harlem, New York. And at the pace I was going, I was on my way. In 1999, we discovered she had lung cancer, and she passed away shortly thereafter. My grandfather had a similar impact on my life. Right after my grandmother's passing, we lost him to prostate cancer. After that, my world began to spiral out of control.

I spent time incarcerated, dropped out of college, had multiple children by different women, went through a divorce, and dealt with a host of things like having bad credit, having nowhere to go, and having my car repossessed. I was completely, from what I felt, far off from my dreams and goals in life. Especially the ones I had promised my grandmother. I kept saying to myself there is no way I can keep living like this. There has to be another way. I realize that most people think that way when facing the pitfalls of life, the hardships, the struggle, and the pain—there has to be another way. But because they can't see themselves in that other way of life, they succumb to their circumstances and simply drift through life, hoping to arrive at death safely.

That's why I always say your circumstances are not your conclusion; instead, the conclusion has to be what you determine, and you determine that by deciding what you want your life to look like.

Albert Einstein once said, "Imagination is the preview of things to come in your life." The issue that I had was I did not realize my imagination was causing me to manifest the things I had going on in my life currently. I was imagining things that I just did not want. So I needed to shift my focus and start to imagine what I did want. Many times, we get stuck because we focus on all of the negative things that are going on in our lives, and by the time we start defining the things we want, it's usually too late.

I knew I didn't want to be broke, homeless, or unhappy. I didn't want to feel weak all the time and float aimlessly through life not feeling valuable. So, as Einstein said, I had to start looking at what I did want. I needed to get a preview of things to come. That can be challenging when you're at a low point, but it's something that must be done if you are going to springboard yourself from where you are to the life you want to live. So, I started seeing myself as someone who had confidence, someone prosperous, someone who people looked up to for inspiration. I began to see myself as this person who stood in front of thousands of people and conducted multimillion-dollar transactions. I began to see myself living where I wanted to live and doing the things that I wanted to do. Not because I had to, but because I wanted to. So, I borrowed $250 from my close friend, and I used it to become a real estate agent.

I couldn't believe that I didn't have $250 at that age.

I remember going into the CEO's office at the real estate agency and saying I appreciate the bagels and the juice, but I can't continue with this training because you guys are talking about commission, and I need to get paid right away. He looked at me, not realizing how serious I was, and said you have to be kidding me. What do you mean you only have this amount of money? I showed him my bank statement, because it was something I carried around with me for motivation. He said, look, I believe you are going to do well. Choose an office that you want to work at right away, and you can pick up this training in the near future.

I went to the office and got the keys. I was the first person in and the last person to leave every day because I didn't have any place to stay. I slept in the office, took showers at a local gym, and over time I built a successful business selling well into the hundred millions in real estate transactions. I married my beautiful wife, and we had three amazing sons.

What started to happen throughout this journey was I realized I was happy I was doing what I was doing, but it was just a vehicle to get me somewhere else. I wanted to impact and empower and inspire people to live their dreams, but for me to do that, I had to truly live mine. So in 2015, I launched my real estate firm MiLL RE, aka MiLL Real Estate. I wanted to become better, so I started reading books, listening to audio, and absorbing all of the material like a sponge. I didn't like reading books. In fact, I hadn't completed a book since my days in college, but I was intrigued by the stories of how people rose from failure to success or fell from success to failure.

I started reading a book by Les Brown called *Live your Dreams*. There was one quote that stood out to me more than anything else. It said, "You have something special; you have greatness in you." There was something about those words that gave me the strength to start thinking of myself a little differently and to start focusing on what I could be instead of what I was. They gave me a ray of light and a little bit of hope that there was a possibility things could turn around, and at that time, it was all I needed.

When I decided to start my speaking career, one of the incredible early opportunities I had was to become one of the founding members of the Les Brown Institute. Les has always been such an inspiration to me and was the catalyst for helping me discover who I was during the downtimes and the moments when I wanted to quit, so I was very excited.

I remember sitting at my first Les Brown seminar. I drove for two hours to get there. As I watched him on stage, I remember thinking that I would do anything to be in his life. I had no idea how it would happen. I didn't have the connections, and I didn't know anyone who knew him personally. The only thing I did know was what I wanted. Back then, one of the opportunities at the Les Brown Institute was to be picked out of two hundred people to speak in front of him.

I remember telling myself, "Oh, I don't need to do that. I'm going to the Institute to learn how to talk. Others are better than me anyway. I need more work. I'll sit this one out. I'll take a picture with him and sit back." I told myself that I wasn't ready yet and that I'd get another chance some other time. But it bothered me every night when I went to sleep, because I knew deep down I wasn't taking the leap because I was afraid. I knew it was a once in a lifetime opportunity to meet my mentor and show him that I truly wanted to inspire people. I also knew that there were millions of people that would die for that chance, and here I was passing it off. What I dreamed about was staring right in my face, and the only obstacle in my way was fear. I was looking for a perfect opportunity. I was looking for someone to call me and say, "I have Les Brown here. Come meet him."

I dug deep. I had to submit a video to enter the competition. It was the first video I ever put together, and to my surprise, I won the opportunity to speak in front of Les. It was the first time I spoke in front of an audience. Les hugged me when I finished speaking and told me that we had a lot of work to do together. I walked off the stage with wobbly knees, cold hands, and a dry throat, but I was inspired because I decided to face my fears and take action. Since that moment, I've been blessed to have Les as a father figure, and I've been able to get advice from the greatest speaker of our time. But none of that would have happened if I had remained paralyzed by inaction and waited to take action. In 2018, I launched the consulting firm Jermain Miller Consulting that trains and motivates coaches and helps people become the greatest version of themselves.

If your self-confidence has been down due to loss, lack, depression, setbacks, or adversity, or if your life has lost its meaning, this book will show you how to break through self-imposed limitations and redesign your future so that you can achieve your goals and be happy. If you have ever wondered how to change your situation when it doesn't look the way you want it to or how to remain focused on your goals and dreams and stop being a victim of your circumstances, *Wake Up & Win: How to Reach Your Goals and Live The Life of Your Dreams* provides proven tips that can help.

When you read this book, you will learn how to make confident decisions that will move you closer to your dreams, despite what may be going on in your life right now. It will show you how to deal with the negative and argumentative inner conversations that surface when you finally decide to go after what you want, and that can keep you from moving forward. If you are struggling to take action to make your goals and dreams a reality, this book will give you proven strategies that can propel you forward.

You no longer have to be a victim of your past. Regardless of where you are in life at this moment, if you are still breathing, you can break free of the chains that have held you captive, but first, you must wake up and win!

CHAPTER 1

What Do You Want?

*We get in life what we don't want because we
never decide what we do want.*

– Jermain Miller

Defining What You Want Too Late

When asked on his deathbed what he would do if he could live his life
over again, activist and playwright George Bernard Shaw said, "I'd like
to be the person I could have been but never was." He realized too late
that he spent his entire life doing things he really didn't want to do. He
came into the knowledge of what he truly wanted when there was no
chance for him to do something about it.

A small majority of people won't have to wait until they're on their
deathbeds to think about their dreams. They're the ones who wake up
and realize their true purpose. They know every moment of the day is
an opportunity to achieve the good they desire. They know what they
want. Unfortunately for the vast majority of people, there will be a
moment when they're faced with a situation similar to George Bernard
Shaw's. At that point, all the time to accomplish dreams quickly
dwindles down to nothing as the final seconds go by.

No one knows the exact moment the clock will stop, yet so many of us behave like we're unfamiliar with how precious time is. Every day, we approach our dreams or the things we want for ourselves nonchalantly. We say, "I'll get around to taking care of myself, building my dreams, and going after my goals soon, but right now there are just so many things to focus on that are much more important." We tell ourselves that we'll do it tomorrow or that we'll start fresh next week, next month, or next year because we want a clean slate and for everything to be perfect before we make the move to go after what we really want to do, be, and have, but we never seem to get around to it.

Why is that? Well, we sorta have an idea of what we want, but because we don't know how or when it's going to happen, or we tell ourselves that we have to see how things will turn out first, we wait to make a full commitment. "I don't want to leave where I am now until I see how I am gonna get there," we say. Then somehow, we convince ourselves with our self-talk to spend years chasing things we don't really want, and we enter a vicious cycle of procrastinating, resisting, arguing, and complaining about the things that happen. We're met with weak challenges that we magnify, and that takes all of our time and energy because we have a false idea that they are just too hard to overcome. Depleted by these fights, we throw in the towel. What we did not want was strong enough to keep us from making the commitment to what we did. Even though we wanted the best things in life, because we failed to think positively, constructively and clearly, our thoughts became doubts. They were random and uncontrolled, and that, in turn, became what manifested in our lives. Every day that we don't define our dreams or act on our goals, we're taking them for granted. If we continue to do that when we reach the end of it all, we'll beg to have a few more hours to accomplish them so we can be all that we've desired. Or, as George Bernard Shaw said, to be the people we could have been but never got the "chance" to be.

So, What Do You Want?

It's an incredible question to be asked, but even more incredible for us to ask ourselves. Our response is usually based on the things we don't want that are happening in our lives at the moment. "I know what I want," we say, and if our lives are not what we believe they should be, we spend all of our time explaining why we put up with a life we don't like. However, the results we get determine what we truly desire. Earl Nightingale once said everyone is the sum total of their own thoughts, and that we are where we are because that's exactly where we really want to be, whether we will admit to it or not.

Everything we have now, we have not because we feel we should but because it's what we've settled for. We say, "I'll take this, but if something else better comes along, I'll take that." Where we live, the car we drive, where we shop, who we hang around, the type of job and career we choose, and most importantly, our goals and dreams are all the products of our thinking, and they are what we really wanted. They may not be what we talked about to our friends or what we discussed with our families. The reality is what we intended to do was one thing, and what we settled for is often something completely different.

If you are ever going to end up where you want to be, you must be very clear and very specific. A wish, daydream, or mere hope won't work. You must define your wants, desires, and dreams. You have to be conscious of these definitions—that means you know them and you've spent time thinking, planning, and dreaming of them regardless of any obstacles, setbacks, or challenges. Your definitions will pull you, push you, and provoke you to get to your goals.

When Napoleon Bonaparte said, "I see only my objective. The obstacle must give way," he was focused on one thing, and that was his clearly defined objective. His objective was his goal, his dream, his idea. It was the thing he wanted to accomplish regardless of the circumstances. When you have an objective in life, it's the only thing you know, and you spend time with it daily. You don't allow circumstances, setbacks or adversities to get in the way, because you understand that all of those things are a part of the process. When we do allow circumstances to get in the way of our objective, it's because we know the definitions of all the things we don't want all too well. We can describe them with accuracy, imagine them in detail, and paint beautiful pictures of loss and lack all day long. We talk about it to everyone that will listen. This takes up the space and energy required for us to focus on the good things we want. We have to stop focusing on what we don't want. We have to let that go and let go of things like excuses, blame, regret, and all the reasons why certain decisions were made or not made that led us to where we are today and choose to only see our objective.

The human mind dislikes change. That's why letting go of things that have run their course in our lives is usually a challenge. It's easier to focus on what we don't want and harder to focus on what we do. The problem is in order for us to move forward, we can't keep looking at what we don't want. Right now, pull out a piece of paper and decide on the things that are no longer beneficial to you and that you no longer want in your life. Make a list of them. Until these things are dismissed and the consequences of their release are completed, your new desires, ideas and dreams will not stick, and you'll never have the life that you want.

Do I Want To?

Asking "Do I want to?" is the only prerequisite for making a decision. You have to want to get off of the fence if you're ever going to get the things you want out of life. Far too often, we're so preoccupied with what life looks like now that we don't make the changes we need for our future. This is a huge mistake. If you've made mistakes in the past that have caused you to deal with consequences today, continuing to look at things the same way won't change your situation. Here's what I want you to know. Where you are now due to those mistakes is only temporary. It's not permanent. Your current circumstances are actually making it possible for you to do what you really want to do because they are making you uncomfortable where you are. The discomfort you feel is just a constant nagging reminder that there is something more, something better, something greater than where you are now.

Ask yourself, do I want to:

- Change my future
- Look at my life as it could be
- Write down my goals
- Spend time working on my dream
- Believe in me when no one else does
- Focus on my opportunities
- Not care if I don't have the money to get started
- Take action

It's difficult to have faith in something you want but can't see, and if you're surrounded by things that are the opposite of what you believe you can have, they can pull you away from what you want. Asking "Do I want to" helps you focus on where you are now, and it helps you determine where you want to be.

Don't Drift

William James, the father of American psychology, once said, "If you wish to be rich, you will be rich; if you wish to be learned, you will be learned; if you wish to be good, you will be good. Only you must, then, really wish these things, and wish them with exclusiveness, and not wish at the same time a hundred other incompatible things just as strongly."

It's that simple. If there is something that you want, you have to aim at it. There has to be a specific target, and you have to be certain it's what you want. In the process of getting what you want, you can't entertain conflicting and opposing thoughts, because they can be overpowering and take you away from what you really want.

The reason we don't get what we want is we slightly drift away from our goals every day, and after so long, it gets harder to align. When we drift, we create negative habits like spending the major portion of our days thinking about all of the things that are going wrong. These habits become hard to break. We continue to drift while we wait for our circumstances to get better or for an opportunity to come. We move further away from what we want as we wait for the job to give us a raise, to win the lotto, or for a great life to fall out of the sky so we can live the life we've always dreamed about. We tell ourselves that we will endure suffering in the present, because if we just drift along and wait, things will be fine one day. Drifting leads to a victim mentality instead of a victor mentality. It gives us a million reasons why we can't take responsibility for the lives we've created.

There is a brighter future for you, but you have to prepare for it. The future will not be certain for you until you become certain about it. What we must understand is that every day of our lives is either a success or a failure. There's no in-between. Either we are acting with authority in our worlds, or our worlds will act with authority on us. When we don't know what we want, we spend a lifetime targeting with uncertainty—aimless, foggy goals that lead to days filled with unproductive activities, which in turn leads to a bunch of excuses instead of a life of achievement. Our dominant daily mental attitude is the main reason everything comes into our lives. Thoughts of fear, failure, discouragement, and indecision cause us to drift away from our goals. We have to take responsibility, define an objective, and focus on it alone to create the life we want to live.

Step Forward

One day while sitting down with a client, I listened as she went on and on about where she had failed. She was only twenty-five years old. She complained about all the reasons she wasn't getting ahead. Her biggest challenges were her assumption of what she should have accomplished and what people thought about where she should be in her life. When she finished, I asked her how old she would be in three years. She said she'd be twenty-eight years old. So, I told her, "Here is where you are, there is where you want to be. If you don't get going now, there will be things that fill up the gap in those three years that will make it tougher for you than it is now." I told her that if she gave herself three years of unbroken focus on her goals, she would achieve the life that she wanted and be where she wanted to be.

Abraham Maslow once said people either step forward into growth or step back into safety. Most of our failures come from pulling back right before we're about to take a leap into something we want to do.

When this happens, we never get to do the things we want, and we fail before we start. Life doesn't require anyone to take action or succeed. No one will wake you up every morning and ask you how close you are to achieving your dreams. No one will hold you accountable, but there is a life you will reap for the compounding inefficiency you sow. If you don't want to live a mediocre, undesirable, and unfulfilling life, you need to stop complaining and step forward.

How to Get What You Want

Our ideas and beliefs must be high and positive if we are to receive the things we want. We have to believe in ourselves and anticipate that we will achieve great things. Our expectation needs to be like the hungry lion waiting for its prey. The lion expects to catch its food at any moment. He's patient. He knows what he wants and believes he'll eventually get it. Like the lion, the higher your expectation, the more you draw the success you desire to you. To achieve success, you have to stop settling, know what you want, and set your bar high.

You know that you don't want to:

- fail
- be unhappy
- be lonely
- be in a bad relationship
- struggle
- be like your parents

If your thoughts are dominated by the things you don't want, you'll attract those things into your life, and you'll have no room to create the things you do want. In turn, you'll settle for a lot less than you can have. Shockingly, if you ask most people what they want for themselves, they'll give you a laundry list of what they don't want instead. In the meantime, they say "I'm waiting" for:

- things to ease up a bit
- things to get better
- an opportunity to pass my way
- a bag of money to appear
- for my job to give me a raise
- to win the lottery

These are not clearly defined goals or desires, and because they're not, life becomes a clear reflection of an undefined image.

Getting what you want starts with the idea that you can have it. It's like planting a seed in the ground. You know the moment you plant the seed that by nature's process, what you plant is what you get. When tomorrow or next week comes, and there is no harvest, you don't go to the ground and say, "Hey, harvest, where are you? You're not here yet? Let me dig up this seed I planted. This dream thing isn't working." No, in order to get that harvest you have to cultivate the soil, make sure there's enough sunlight and water, and keep weeds from taking up residence in your garden. Your dreams, ideas, and goals are your seeds. You have to cultivate your mind with positive thoughts to manifest them. You have to make sure there is enough sunlight, which means no negativity, and you have to keep everything watered, which means staying away from anything that doesn't help you grow.

Decide What You Want to Do

People spend their entire lives doing things they don't want to do only to end up in the latter years complaining about why the things they really wanted never appeared. Avoid this costly mistake by making clear-cut decisions. There can't be any wavering back and forth or part-time wants. You have to know what you want so that even if you can't see the finish line, you'll still believe that what you want is worth going for. You have to make a full-out commitment. Most of the time, fear and ignorance keep us from making a decision concerning what we want to do. If we don't decide what we want, we can spend a lifetime being the victim and getting pushed around by life and people who do know what they want. The dreams we have and the goals we want to accomplish require our full focus and an all-out effort.

Here are some things you can do to get clear about what you want:

Write It Down

It's important to write goals and ideas down. When we write them down, we're writing the blueprint for our dreams. We're allowing ourselves to not focus on things as they are but as they could be. It also gives us a higher probability of accomplishing them. Writing things down gives you a higher chance of you accomplishing what you want because there is accountability.

Make a List and Put What's Important First

Organize your goals into a list then put what's most important to you first. Most people don't reach their goals because they feel they need to accomplish everything on their list right away. They compare goals to checklist items. However, goals are not checklist items. Checklist items are things you know how to do, like drive a car, go to the store, go to work. Goals cause you to grow into a different type of person in order to accomplish them. Your goals should be so large that you are growing, working, dreaming, and believing every day to become the person you need to be in order to get them done. Start by taking one dream, one thought, or one idea and building upon it until it happens. Use all of your energy on it. As you work toward that one dream, you'll find that you no longer give attention to the things you don't want for your life as your goals become the only thing you focus on.

See Yourself in Possession of It Night and Day

One of the biggest challenges we face is our inability to continually see ourselves in possession of what we really want. This is hard to do, but it's the key step in getting what you want. You must see yourself in possession of what you want to have, who you want to be, and what you want to do every day. This is why writing the list down is important because it helps you see what you can have, what you can do, and what you can be. This keeps you focused on getting what you truly desire.

Take Action

You must develop a burning desire to cultivate a definiteness of purpose. This requires a radical change within. It occurs when you determine what you are willing to give in exchange for the life that you want. There is no such thing as something for nothing, so it's important that when you decide what you want, you know that you have to do something in order to get it. That's taking action. How can you improve what you are currently doing in your business, your job, your home? Who could you help, support, or encourage? Where can you go to learn more about what you want to do? What books can you read and what seminars can you attend that can take you to the next level? These are some of the ways you can take action to exchange what you have to get what you want.

Before you move on to the next chapter, I want you to stop and think about what you truly want. Don't think about what you believe you could have if things were easy or about what you see others with, but instead what you want deep down inside. Your circumstances will only change when you change what you want. If you want the new life you dream about, you have to change your thoughts and keep them changed. But in order to do that, you have to decide what you want.

Ask yourself the following questions to decide what you want out of life:

1. If you could live your life over again and be free from all types of fear, what are five things you would do?

2. If you were financially independent, what is the first thing you would do?

3. Write a list of five things that you want. Write the list as though it were impossible for you to fail.

4. What's the most important thing for you to accomplish from the list of five things you want?

5. What feeling would accomplishing the thing you want most give you?

CHAPTER 2

Inner Conversations

If there is no enemy within, the enemy without can do us no harm.

– African Proverb

The Wake-Up

It is 4:45 in the morning and my alarm is ringing. It's dark. The house is quiet and it's quiet outside. I've made a commitment, as I've done many times in the past, to start my new routine, be more disciplined, and set higher goals, and now it's time to live up to it. How can my life become better? How can I have more? How can I overcome these challenges in life? These are the real questions, and they haunt me every day. I look over at my wall and zero in on something I have written about fear. It's part of a quote from Robert Ingersoll that says, "Fear is the dungeon of the mind to which it runs and hides and seeks seclusion. Fear brings on superstition, and superstition is the dagger with which hypocrisy assassinates the soul."

I lie in bed, knowing the longer I stay, the easier it'll be for me to close my eyes and listen to those all too familiar inner conversations that roam around my mind persuading me to put everything off until tomorrow by explaining the benefits of hitting the snooze button. The comfort of being where I am right now makes me want to forget my commitment, but I know if I do, I'll be tormented by the laziness and excuses that have been producing poor results. I'm tired of my own empty promises.

* * *

Have you ever wanted freedom from limitations? Freedom from your problems? Freedom from fear? Every time we seem to get an idea of what we want to do with our lives, our minds wander to places and circumstances that are less important. Distracted, we become spectators because we never start on our goals, and then it becomes a cycle. Maybe it's because the less important stuff seems easier to get distracted by, and maybe we feel if we get involved in that we can feel like we are accomplishing something. Maybe it's that small inner voice that says today you don't have to do it. Nothing bad will happen.

I'm sure in the past, we have all said, "This time is different. I'm committed not to live with the state of mind that allows self-imposed limitations to rule my life. I'm going to eliminate procrastination and quit not giving life my all." Because living that way holds us back, and the truth be told, it's tiring—which is frustrating. But talking one way and doing something else becomes a problem and a struggle when the time for action comes and fear kicks in. But what are we afraid of? And why have we been so afraid so long?

Sometimes, we've had enough of the way our lives are, and we know we want to give more and do more, but we remain the same because we tell ourselves that we at least have a degree of comfort. Things are frantic, but we tell ourselves it's okay, and we feel safe. What about fear?

Have you ever told yourself you can't do what you want to because of something else, but it was only you being too afraid that you'll fail in front of everyone? Do you ever find yourself saying that you have to start big or not start at all? Go hard or go home, we say, but we end up staying home. What about the money? The small voice says, "Don't you need more than what you have to get started with your dream? Since you don't have any, shouldn't you wait until you do? What about the perfect opportunity? Shouldn't you just wait until that appears?"

How many times have you broken commitments, not to others but to yourself, and become so accepting of failure and letting yourself down that breaking commitments and failing became a habit that you are secretly okay with? Our lives will be as small or as large as our controlling inner talk. Oftentimes we talk ourselves out of the lives we could create. Changes don't just happen. They occur because we change what we say about what we can do and what we're facing. Ask yourself, are your current daily inner conversations building you up or tearing you down? Your mental talks will either encourage you to go back to sleep and stay trapped in a nightmare or cause you to wake up and tackle your dreams.

What are Inner Conversations?

Have you ever thought about the conversations you have with yourself every day? The nature of these talks will determine where you end up. These are the inner conversations we have with ourselves. They are the positive and negative, conscious and unconscious conversations we secretly have daily that affect what we think, say and do. It's the conversations we have with ourselves in private, not the ones we have in public with our friends, family, and associates, that determine how high or low we go. Sadly, these powerful conversations we have are mostly argumentative. They constantly tell us what we shouldn't or can't do, and who we shouldn't be. They make us unhappy about who we are and what we can accomplish. Despite this fact, we become comfortable with these inner conferences, and they become similar to the casual conversations we have with a close friend we fully trust with our darkest fears. Our inner conversations can push us toward success, or they can keep us in a corner in fear. They can push us to greatness or talk us into a life unfulfilled. They can stop any forward progress in our lives even when we know we deserve more and need to make some changes. They're tiny self-defeating talks that we allow ourselves to be sold on. The intensity of these talks leads us to create situations we don't want and leaves us staring at circumstances we'd rather not deal with.

Anything we say to ourselves often enough will seek expression in our lives. In most cases, it's through our physical bodies. It will show outwardly by the look on our faces, the posture of our bodies, the lack of confidence in our walk, and the uncertainty in how we speak and communicate. It also can create a sickness that was never there, death when there should be life, poverty that shouldn't remain, and fear instead of courage. When we fail to master what we say to ourselves, it will master us and keep us from reaching our dreams. If we are ever going to change our lives, we must first start with changing our inner talks. Every day we're doing one of two things. We're either talking ourselves into poverty, misery, and failure or talking ourselves into heights of achievement and creating a life of abundance, success, and happiness. Our futures will be created by our inner conversations. We have to plant success and great things in our minds through the positive words we say to ourselves repeatedly. Positive and negative conversations cannot occupy our minds at the same time. One or the other will dominate. One dominates by default, which means we don't have to do anything—it's automatic. The other dominates by repetition, which means you have to constantly speak positively. Whether positive or negative, the choice is yours, but you cannot speak one way and reap the fruit that's opposite of what you speak. You have the freedom to choose what you say. When you choose to say positive things, you'll attract more positive situations into your life. One powerful positive thing you can say to yourself is "I will no longer accept any negative outside circumstance or condition. They don't have any dominance in my life."

Something struck me while I was watching an episode of *National Geographic* that showed a bison giving birth. Now, before the bison went into labor, coyotes had surrounded a member of the herd, but the bison was able to make a run for it. While this was happening, somehow, one of the pregnant bison was able to veer off, hide, and give birth. The show's narrator said that within two to three hours the baby bison would be strong enough to run with its herd and even run away from the coyote. Its mother was aware of the danger surrounding her, so she stuck around and pushed the baby to get it moving. At that moment it dawned on me that the baby bison is just like our dreams. When we have a dream or a goal, our inner conversations have to be like the mother bison pushing us toward their realization. What we say to ourselves has to be positive, and we need to take action fast, or our dreams will get eaten by the coyotes which are our negative inner conversations. We can't lay around thinking that we can live without constant positive self-talk. We have to get going speaking positive and affirming messages to ourselves immediately. Think of yourself as the big bison and your inner conversations as the baby bison and the coyote. If you speak life to yourself, your dreams and your goals, they will eventually live. If not, the negative coyote conversations will have you in a corner fighting for your life.

Knowing What to Do

In William Shakespeare's play, *The Merchant of Venice,* the character Portia says to her maid Nerissa, "If to do were as easy as to know what were good to do . . ." In other words, if doing were as easy as knowing, we all would live the lives of our dreams, be everything we want to be, and achieve all that we desire. We find it more difficult to do than to know what to do because of our self-talk that turns us into prosecuting attorneys against ourselves. Most of the time we have an idea of the things we know we want to do, like:

- Change the world
- Live a better life
- Start a business
- Make a lot of money
- Finish school
- Buy a dream home for our family
- Get healthy even in the midst of setbacks and hardships

The challenge we have is in the conflicting conversations that talk us out of our dreams. We know what we want to do, we know how we want to live, we know we want love and happiness, but we beat ourselves down and allow self-imposed limitations to hinder our progress. We small talk and pep talk ourselves into negative thinking.

Shakespeare said, "Our doubts are traitors and make us lose the good we oft might win by fearing to attempt."

What he meant was we don't fail at doing the thing we want to, we fail because we never actually do a thing. We don't even attempt, because our inner conversations make us believe that where we are is better than where we want to be. Sometimes if we do make the attempt, we go flying immediately to achieve a high goal because we've talked ourselves into believing that getting everything at once is success. When we don't reach that dream right away, we come crashing down, and our inner conversations tell us that we should never try to get up again.

Have you ever found yourself repeating:

- I don't have the money.
- I have too many bills.
- It's not the right time.
- My life is too hectic and it's just too hard.
- You don't understand, I grew up in a bad environment.
- I had too many things to overcome.
- I don't know how I would ever be able to achieve that.
- Someone like me doesn't deserve it.
- This is just the way life is and I have to accept it.
- There's not much for me to live for because bad things have happened to me.
- I have to go through bad things in order to get to good things.

Moving forward in life is going to require you to no longer entertain weak, harmful, negative inner conversations and thoughts about yourself. You can't bring about strong, beautiful, harmonious conditions speaking like that. Most of us can agree that we've allowed our negative inner conversations to talk ourselves down to what we call reality and make us believe we can't achieve our goals. We believe instead that something is blocking us or that there is some dark force doing things that are stopping us, because we're unaware of the damage we're doing to ourselves. You can, in fact, achieve your dreams. However, you must understand that to be something, you must do something, and the doing is a change in your inner conversations.

First, you'll need to change your inner conversations from negative to positive, and to do that, you have to be in a neutral, receptive mindset. If your mind isn't open, it doesn't matter what you tell yourself—your negative self-talk will remain dominant. You'll never accomplish anything until you can be receptive to positive words about yourself. You have to learn the difference between negative and positive self-talk. You must be honest, truthful, and decent with yourself before you can change your inner conversations from negative to positive. To change your inner conversations, you must go from discussing what you can't do to what you can, from "I won't" to "I will" from "I should" to "I can." When you change your self-talk, it will help you change the way you perceive yourself. After your perception changes, opportunities for you to grow into the person you need to be to achieve your goals will begin to manifest.

I'm No Longer Speaking That

If you want to be free from the past or any struggle, you have to know what has caused it. Most often, what you see in your life has been caused by what you failed to speak. The word "no" is tremendously powerful when we use it in our inner conversations. When we don't fight our negative inner conversations with the word "no," we begin to lose power over our lives. When you say no to what you don't want, you will finally be able to break free and move toward peace. Not saying no makes life difficult and puts us in places that are unpleasant. However, the word "no" spoken in our minds eliminates all the hurdles and obstacles in our lives. It's clear and direct.

"No. I'm no longer accepting this."

"No. I'm no longer going to speak this way."

"No. I'm no longer going to allow this negative talk to keep me from living my life."

"No. I'm no longer allowing people that take me away from my goal to hang around me."

Just like the most expensive car must have periodic tune-ups or it will fail to function properly, our inner conversations must be maintained. While a car may need gas frequently to give it energy, our conversations need fuel on a regular basis for us to function at our maximum potential.

Here are some things you can do to fuel your inner conversations:

Cleanse Your Inner Conversations Daily

Don't let your negative inner conversations overpower you. Be proactive. Make it a habit every day to speak kind, positive and affirming words to yourself.

Pay Attention to What You Say

Take time each day to search for and speak positive, goal-oriented words that take you toward the destination of your choice.

Don't Contaminate the Atmosphere with Negative Conversations

Negative conversations pollute the atmosphere. If people are around you are speaking negatively, don't become their garbage can or a human magnet. If you begin to say something negative, don't finish the sentence. Instead, replace it with something positive.

If Your Mind Is in Need of Repair Take It to The Right Mechanic

If you're not in a good space, get around people who can help and who will affirm the good, speak positively about where you are going, and whose intentions are not to see you stuck or worse off than where you are. It's important to remember that affirmation without discipline is delusional. Many people live unfulfilled lives because while they affirm the good for their lives, they don't discipline themselves with the action that's needed. Sometime around 600 BC, Lao Tso said that when the sage goes into the jungle, he carries no sword or spear. He is not afraid of a javelin or tooth of a rhinoceros because there is in him no place where these can enter. In other words, he conditioned his mind based on his inner conversations. He built an immunity to the things going on around him. He disciplined himself to take action with the repetition of positive and affirming self-talk.

Changing Conversations

I remember getting on a plane one day when the walkway was completely crowded. By the time I got to my seat, there were still a lot of people behind me, so I thought I'd be late reaching my destination. The flight attendant announced that for us to arrive on time, we'd need to get moving in seven minutes. I thought that was impossible. There were just too many people. But the crew had a system, and it started with the conversations they had with each other and the belief that if they got what they needed to do finished quickly, they'd get us to our destination on time.

I want you to imagine you're a big plane that's getting ready for takeoff. You're going to the destination of your dreams. Everything you've ever wanted will be yours when you get there, but before you take off, there are some important things that need to happen for you to take flight. To get to your dreams, you have to clear your runway from all negative and toxic conditions, like the "I can't" attitude, failure mentality, victim mindset, negative environments, baggage, drama, and any other obstacles in the way and maintain positive communication with the control tower—which is your mind.

Right before you take off and gain speed, you need constant positive communication to yourself, also called positive self-talk. You'll be met with resistance in the form of challenges, obstacles, and adversity when you're going after your goals, but, as the pilot of this aircraft, you can't say, "You know what? Let's pump the brakes and make a U-turn. It's not a good idea for me to fly right now," because you'll never get to your destination. There are people on board waiting for you to achieve your dreams so you can inspire them to live theirs. There are people that need you to get to your destination, because by you getting there, they get to theirs as well.

Let's start new conversations that allow us to take off and fly. Let's talk ourselves to our dreams and our goals instead of away from them. Sell yourself on the idea that you can build the life you really want to live and finally get off the runway. Today is the day you'll stop running in circles on the runway while hoping, wishing, and praying that you'll reach your destination one day. Today is the day you'll lift off.

Aristotle said, "We are what we repeatedly do. Excellence, then, is a habit."

Today, I want you to begin the habit of having positive inner conversations. Only speak of the things you want to happen, the life you want to live, and the things you want to do. See yourself as whole, perfect, strong, powerful, and loving. Hold conversations with yourself about all the things you've overcome and how your life has changed for the better. Smile at the things you once thought were challenging and tough to overcome. See yourself where you want to be. Take a trip to the life of your dreams in your imagination. See yourself there. Talk to yourself from the place that you want to be. How do you feel? What are your thoughts? How confident are you now, in the place you've dreamed of reaching? This is why affirmation is so powerful. It cancels out the negative self-talk.

I remember having a conversation with myself in the midst of what I thought at the time was a trying season. I had a conversation with the person I wanted to be and the person I did not want to become. I asked the person I didn't want to be how he ended up where he was. His response was that he was going through so much in life that it was a nightmare. He said his desire for the things he wanted was not strong enough to help him overcome, and he just couldn't seem to talk his way to where he wanted to be. The person I wanted to be was someone I admired; he was successful, happy, and doing all the things I would love to do. I asked him how he ended up where he was. His response was that he was going through so much that his life was also a nightmare, but that the things he wanted to do were so much greater that it pulled him through. That successful self said to me, "Remember all those things you are going through? Remember how many times you said, 'I quit' and 'I can't take this anymore?' The person I am is who you would have given up on. All of the things you were worried about don't even matter." Go to where you want to be in life and talk to yourself from there.

Don't allow your inner conversations to cause you to doubt yourself and keep you trapped in a false nightmare. Change your inner conversations by transforming your thoughts. The questions below can help you unearth the good things already present in yourself and in your life. Your answers can help you press the reset button on your thoughts so that you can have better, more productive inner conversations.

Ask yourself the following questions to change your inner conversations from negative to positive:

1. If your success depended on changing your inner conversations, what three new changes could you make today?
2. Imagine you've achieved everything you desire. List three new conversations you would have with yourself daily as this person.
3. Today is the last day for you to start your new business, finish school, start a new health regimen, or get a raise. What positive inner conversations would you have with yourself to achieve these goals?
4. If you knew you were close to achieving everything you wanted, what three things would you say to yourself every day as you move closer to your goals?
5. If you didn't have to worry about what people would say, what new conversations would you have with yourself?
6. If you didn't have to worry about money, what new conversations would you have with yourself about the things you can do?

CHAPTER 3

The Truth Despite Appearances

Your circumstances may be uncongenial, but they shall not long remain so if you but perceive an ideal and strive to reach it.

– James Allen

Zebra Story

I watched an interesting show about how zebras migrate the other day. Every year, large herds move from Kenya to Botswana in what's said to be one of the largest migrations of mammals in the world. Knowing that the land where they are is drying up due to the change in seasons, the zebras head for greener pastures, but to get there, they have to deal with some extreme challenges and obstacles. Their journey is a tough one because they're easy prey for hungry lions, cheetahs, and leopards that are all waiting to eat them.

When the zebras reach the Nile River, they have to make a huge decision. They hesitate before entering the water. They know from previous experience that there are crocodiles lurking quietly in the river. I'm sure something inside of them told them to turn back to avoid the crocodiles. But maybe the thought of turning around and going back to deal with adversity again only to get back to land that was completely dry just wasn't worth it. As the zebras passed through the water, I thought, wow, these zebras really have a goal they're willing to reach at any cost. Then, something happened. As the water rose and they went in deeper, the crocodiles appeared. These crocodiles were so smooth and so graceful they seemed to glide effortlessly through the water. Some of them had not eaten for months.

The zebras slowed down and began to focus on what was around them instead of using that same energy to move forward quickly. Instinct pushed most of them forward, but some became afraid and only focused on the thing they feared, so their fears became their realities and they were eaten by the hungry crocodiles. As I studied the zebras and the crocodiles, it dawned on me that the crocodiles didn't pop up in front of the zebras. Instead, they appeared on the sides and from behind. The appearance of those scary crocodiles made the zebras lose sight of their goal.

Henry Ford once said, "You only see the obstacles when you lose sight of the goal." That's really the way life is. As we set off to achieve our goals, all of our ideas and dreams are out in front of us. Along our journey, life happens, and if we're not clear about what we are aiming at, if the end goal isn't well defined, we will lose sight of it completely and even begin to question whether we really wanted what we were going after in the first place. Sometimes we think of taking our eyes off the goal and stopping, because it's too overwhelming or we think waiting forever to make a decision won't hurt or cost us that much in the long term. We start to spend too much time thinking about all the things that are around us, believing that we can somehow give all of our energy to what distracts us and still get to our dreams, but it doesn't work that way.

Our dreams must be larger than what we see around us at the moment, especially if what we see is not what we want, like being broke, failure, sickness or not achieving our dreams and being unhappy. Whether you reach your destiny or not will be determined by your ability to see yourself reaching your goal and having the things that you want. When you can do this, your dreams will become magnets that pull you through the hard times.

The zebras knew danger surrounded them, but they pushed through the water anyway because they knew one thing was certain. If they stopped, they'd be overtaken by the crocs. Although they knew it was challenging, they pushed through the water and kept fighting because their goal to migrate to greener pastures was larger than the crocodiles that wanted to eat them and the struggle to swim through the currents in the river. Like the zebras, for many of us, we make it through the lions, cheetahs and leopards of life, and we get to the water. The moment we are there, we either make the decision to commit going forward achieving our dreams, or we start to overanalyze and become paralyzed by the process, so consumed by fear that we quit and the crocodiles of life overtake us. Many of us get through the obstacles and hurdles, but when the intensity starts turning up, we start saying maybe this prosperity is not what we really wanted. When we're met with resistance, throwing in the towel is our first choice and we tell ourselves:

- It's too hard for me to handle.
- This is not what I wanted.
- Why do I have to deal with this?
- What's the use?
- I'll get to my dreams another time.

Every year, we're attacked by crocodiles in the form of adversity, stress, fear or even our own self-imposed limitations. We make commitments, resolutions to create the life we want, and we become inspired by thoughts of doing something great. But the appearance of circumstances we don't want distracts and overpowers us, and we can't seem to recover the positive thoughts about what we really want for ourselves. Yes, your circumstances may rise as high as the water does to the noses of the zebra, but the truth of your desires and the life you really want to live has to outweigh the appearance of your current situation if you are ever going to achieve the good that you desire.

We have the power to think positive thoughts about our ability to achieve our dreams, but doing so takes more effort and concentration than it does to dwell on the hard times we're going through. For many of us, the life we desire won't materialize the moment we start thinking about it. We'll have to dig deep, be very clear, and decide to see what we want to see instead of seeing things as they are. This means a persistent, firm determination to think what we want to think regardless of all outer evidence to the contrary. The reason things get difficult and we get stuck is because we lose faith in what we want, and we no longer persist in the assumption that we can have it. The person who sees what they want regardless of what appears will someday experience outwardly what they have so faithfully seen within.

We have to become aware that where we currently are has nothing to do with our dreams or our purpose, and know that the way that our lives look the moment we decide to make a change is not our truth or reality. We must hold tight to our ideals and the image we have for our lives and never lose sight of them, because we can only confidently walk in the right direction when we believe we can get there without a doubt. Only when we can look at crocodiles as distractions that will not destroy us can we understand and discover the truth despite appearances.

Get Out of Your Own Way

We get in our own way when we don't allow the universe's plans to run their course. Sometimes we are our own crocodiles. We want to control the process. We want to make a straight path to our destination and get there untouched, but since we don't know how, where, or when our dreams will manifest, fear overtakes us. Every time we waver in faith, we kill our dreams. Every time we look at the crocs knowing what they are, we fear them more than we relish our dream. In this state, we get paralyzed and we don't move. We have to remember that the zebras that make it are the ones that don't stop, even though they're afraid. To know your truth is to be absolutely sure and confident. It affords incomparable satisfaction. It is the only solid ground in a world of doubt, conflict and danger. Every action that is not in line with your truth, whether through ignorance or design, will result in failure.

Challenges will come in life. This is all a part of the process, but worrying, procrastinating, and becoming anxious when things don't happen in the time we feel they should only delays us from getting to our goal. There's a process for achieving our dreams. One, we have to connect to our dreams so tightly that it creates an impenetrable shield that will sweep away every kind of fear, doubt, or error in our thinking. Secondly, we must know that the process develops us into who we need to be and reveals to us our level of courage, persistence, and faith. It's the time and labor that's required. Sleepless nights and being broke mixed with belief, hope, ups and downs and persistence are all part of the building process.

Many times, we jump in the water and then ask, "Do I have to swim?" We say, "I can't swim. There are too many crocs in here." Then we ask, "Do I have to figure out my way around them as well?" Yes, it's all part of the process. Do the work and don't focus on what's going on around you. Concentrate on the goal. The goal will pull you through.

When you're digging for gold, getting the gold is the objective. Digging hurts. When there's too much dirt, sometimes people forget the gold. The process is the appearance, and sometimes we pay attention to it too much. We say, "Well, it doesn't look like this is going to happen for me. There can't be any gold this deep," or "The last time I tried it didn't work," or "No one in my family has done this before." We say, "Come on dreams. Where are you?" The anxiety kills us. We'd rather quit than wait. It doesn't work like that. There's a process to this stuff. Your dreams need time. They need time to develop, and they need to get rooted.

Rushing the dream is a manifestation of fear. It's the fear that something will go wrong and that we don't have any control. It's the fear that someone is going to say, "You're doing the wrong thing, try something else." It's disbelief. The only thing that can go wrong in this world is you, by having the wrong mental attitude. Worrying about problems or things that are pressing you for an instant solution will keep you in the mental space of fear and doubt. This is truly when you are out of your greatness.

The process is the work. But we must know that each day we work, we are moving toward something. Every day that you don't see your harvest is not a day to get mad. We don't know what day is designated for it to come in. No one knows the inner workings of the process, that's not our job. Our job is to keep our eyes on the truth and off of how scary things look at the moment. Just because we can't wrap our minds around how things will work out doesn't mean they won't.

A compassionate, wise king wished to help the poor citizens of his land. He refused to hand out unearned benefits, knowing how they corrupt human nature. So he set up bountiful stores of food and clothing at one end of a long, dark valley. All along the trail, he placed straw men, each one more fierce looking than the last. The citizens who dared to face and pass by the fierce figures received their share of the reward. This is what we must do when we are faced with adversity or challenges: we must learn to become aware of their flimsy falseness. If we do this, unwanted emotions disappear like a sandcastle before the waves, and in the process, you will eventually reach a very interesting state. You will no longer have time to fool around with things that used to bother you. You'll ignore them. You'll pass by. You'll smile in amusement at the childish attempts of fear and worry to drag you down. You'll see that they have no power over you, because they can neither take you away from your truth or truly cause you any fear.

Thinking Higher Than the Negative Appearances

When a boxer is going up to fight an opponent that's stronger, looks to be in better shape, and may have a better record, he cannot fight the same way his opponent fights. If he does, he will lose. He must outbox him by a different strategy, and that is the mental strategy. That is knowing that the only way to win will be to fight better mentally. What this means is we can't keep fighting the appearance of things based upon how they look. In order for us to overcome the challenges, we must first know what they are and understand that adversity is always going to be adversity and challenges will always be challenges. Heartbreak, shock, trials—they are all the same. They may come at different points in our lives from different people or places, but they are the same. They don't change. What does change is us. Once we are clear on what they are, we can raise our thinking to rise above them. The level of thinking that caused the circumstances is not the same level of thinking that's going to pull us out.

Likewise with the fighter: If he gets knocked down or if he is losing, he has to change his thinking if he is going to win. For many of us, when we get an idea of the life we want to live, we are not in the financial, physical or mental position to act on it, and, in most cases, that's the only reason we become stagnant. We become angry. We focus too much on our current position and then itemize the excuses. You don't need anything to start moving towards your goals except the knowledge of what you want and the desire to keep moving forward until you achieve it. If you want to be in a different place in life, you have to see yourself there before you get there. If you want to have a better job, complete school, overcome sickness, or break the chains of poverty, you can if you know the truth despite the appearance.

When an architect draws plans, he first sees the images in his mind. He has every detail drawn out line by line in advance. He spends hours in his imagination and has seen the end in mind through visualization before he ever sees the finished product. No matter how many times he changes his plans, he never changes what he wants the end result to be: the manifestation of what he imagined. He doesn't expect something to be built based on a bunch of aimless thoughts, incomplete plans and lack of commitment to the process. He takes his time planning, correcting, thinking and drawing things out. He doesn't lose time waiting for a brighter future to suddenly appear for his ideas to come to pass. Like the architect, you have to, in your own imagination, present the case that you know what your truth is and be determined to confidently advance in the direction of it no matter what is going on in your life right now.

So, what images have you been holding in your mind? What do you visualize? How much time have you spent unconsciously thinking about the things that are manifesting in your life now?

Here's the truth. You can accomplish all you want to accomplish. You have unlimited potential to achieve anything you want. You have a unique destiny and purpose to fulfill while here on this earth, but it's up to you to fulfill it. There are people waiting for you to live your dreams because you're the only one that can inspire them to live theirs. No one knows the darkness you've faced and the struggles you have. They don't see the years of pain and hurt. They only see you hanging in there and trying your best to push through.

The bigger your dreams and the higher your goals, the more important it is for you to change your thoughts toward them. It's time for you to come out of hiding and to walk out of the doors that have held you back. It's time for you to break through walls of over-analysis that have been a barrier to your dreams. So what if everything isn't the way you want it to be. So what if things aren't perfect. So what if you've had some hardships, setbacks, and struggles. The truth is, we have to realize that it starts with us. It starts with confidence in ourselves and the things we say to ourselves. We have to stop being comfortable with the word 'impossible.' We can define the word too well. When we associate our lives with the word 'impossible,' we'll never be able to achieve what we want. Let go of that word and the thinking that comes with it, and replace it with thoughts of what can be possible for you.

Neville Goddard once said, "Assume you are already that which you seek and your assumption, though false, if sustained, will harden into fact." That means right now, things may not look like your truth. In fact, everything may be contrary to it. The low points in some of our lives have lasted so long that we assume having unhappiness, low confidence, and struggling to survive is the way it will always be, so we persist in negative thoughts until they become our reality. The reason things get difficult and we get stuck is because we lose faith and stop persisting in the assumption that we can be what we want to be. We have to believe that despite the negative appearance, we can reach our goals.

The Oak Tree

I found some very motivating information while I was studying oak trees recently. The average lifespan of an oak tree is anywhere between two hundred and fifty to five hundred years, and they grow from fifty to one hundred feet tall. They have two major purposes. The first is to grow to their maximum height and the second is to give more life. In giving more life, they help produce oxygen and acorns, which have the seed of another oak tree inside of them. However, it takes thirty years for an oak tree to produce its first acorn. In the forty-four years that follow, it will continue to produce acorns, but does so inconsistently. It's not until its seventy-fifth year that the oak tree starts to produce acorns regularly. That means it takes forty-five years of additional growth for acorn production to become consistent. The reason the oak tree can't be consistent in its earlier years is because it's not mature. It has to grow to its maximum potential to produce acorns with regularity.

As it grows, the oak tree weathers hurricanes, thunderstorms, and natural disasters. It loses its leaves in the fall and gains them in the spring while still growing to its fullest potential. Like the oak tree, when you're working toward your goals, you sometimes show few visible signs of progress. Your progress may appear very inconsistent on the outside, and people may look at you and say, "You've been working that dream, and this is all you have to show for it? You've been talking about your ideas, but that business you started isn't yielding you anything on a regular basis. You need to give it up. It's not working for you." You may start to question yourself and wonder what's wrong. You've been putting in the time, but some days you're winning, some days you're losing—and all you want is consistency.

One thing about the oak tree is that it does not move. It keeps growing. It stays planted and weathers the storm. It knows that for it to produce with consistency, it has to grow. When your 74th year comes and you want to throw in the towel because the pain of waiting and the appearance of things is too much to bear or the losses seem to outweigh the wins, there has to be something deep down inside of you that helps you muster up your strength and have the courage to say, "No! I'm an oak tree! So what it's seventy-five years in? I have more life left in me." Only then will you be able to give it one more shot, one last go, and start to yield consistent results and live the life you've always wanted to live; you've come to understand there's a truth that sometimes only you can see, despite how your life appears to others.

Overcoming the Appearance

For long periods of time, you've examined the negative appearance of your circumstances and have tried to figure out why you aren't achieving the things you want. Today I want you to shift your focus. Like James Allen says in his groundbreaking book, *As a Man Thinketh*, walk out of the door that's held back your dreams. When you finally walk out, you will find yourself in front of a crowd. What you say won't come out perfectly, but you must go now because there's no better time. When you do, you'll be able to pour out all of your aspirations in front of others. Life is the master teacher. You're in the arena. You're where you need to be, and there is nothing more to teach you. It's time to act. It's time for you to stop being the student. It's time for you to live your dreams.

Life is challenging, but that challenge allows you to grow and become and discover. Your challenges are pushing you to become someone new so you can have what you desire. They're letting you know that this isn't the end and that there's something greater for you. If the bad stuff hadn't happened, what route would you have taken? What things would you have not accomplished because the desire wasn't as strong to see what you wanted manifested? Yes, the pressure is hard, the situation seems unbearable, and doors are being shut tight, but you have to dig your heels in and bring forth the manifestation of your dreams.

You don't need more knowledge, a better education, or more facts. You need to make better use of the knowledge you already have. You have everything within you necessary to do whatever you can conceive and believe, but you have to know that it has to come through you.

When you know that something is yours, regardless of what your life looks like or what anyone says, does, or thinks, it fills you with confidence.

Ask yourself the following questions to identify your crocodiles and to discover your truth despite appearances:

1. What are some crocodiles in your life that you are focused on? Are they keeping you away from your dreams?
2. What are three things you want to happen, but believe no longer will because of how the circumstances in your life appear?
3. What are three things you will commit to this year, no matter what negative things appear in your life?
4. Now that you're aware that you will have challenges in life, what three things will you do when the next challenge arises?
5. What are you willing to do while you are going through your oak tree process?

CHAPTER 4

Waiting to Take Action

*People say nothing is impossible and then spend
all day doing nothing.*

– Unknown

Paralyzed by Inaction

Have you ever asked for more time in the day or said that if you
had twenty-six hours instead of twenty-four that you'd be a lot more
productive? Unfortunately, we only get twenty-four hours. In fact, we
all have the same twenty-four hours to work with, and no matter how
hard we try, it will always be twenty-four hours and nothing more.
We have to become better at using the time we have. In his great book
Rhythms of Life, William E. Bailey tells a story about a man who asks
the universe for more time. The universe responds by telling the man,
"There is no more time. Give me more of you."

During a client coaching session, my client talked about not having
much time to accomplish anything she wanted. She felt like there was
never enough time. She became inspired by the suggestion I gave her to
wake up earlier to get more out of her day. Getting up early is certainly
not the easiest thing to do, especially if you don't have to, but if you're

going to achieve your goals and become successful, getting a head start on the things you want to accomplish is something to consider. She was determined and made the commitment to wake up at 5 am. She said she committed to doing it because she knew all of the benefits of getting a head start, but when I followed up with her a few days later, to my surprise, she told me that she wanted to wait until the following week to begin. She said there were too many things that she had to focus on and that she wanted a clean slate so she could start off fresh before beginning her new discipline. What really happened was she became paralyzed by not taking action.

How many times have you told yourself that you'll start working on your goals and going after your dreams tomorrow, then tomorrow comes and you say you'll get started next week or next month or closer to the end of the year? How many times have you told yourself that you need to wait for the perfect opportunity to take shape so that you can ease your way into taking action? Often, when the day finally comes and it's time for us to take the first step, we can't because we've become paralyzed by inaction and because too many other distractions have taken action on us so we can't make a move. Every day we're either moving toward what we want, or we're delaying ourselves the opportunity to achieve our goals. The problem is we're thinking too much instead of acting.

Busy Non-Action

Seneca once said, "The greatest loss of time is delay and expectation, which depend upon the future. We let go of the present, which we have in our power, and look forward to that which depends upon chance and so relinquish a certainty for an uncertainty." In other words, if you leave your life up to chance, chances are it's not going to turn out the way you want.

For many of us, the great philosopher's words ring true. Have you ever found yourself constantly delaying what's important to deal with less important things? When this happens, there is action being taken, but very little time is spent moving toward anything specific. When we get tied up and realize what we're doing has little value, we often try to refocus but eventually fall back into the trap of just being busy instead of being busy building the life of our dreams with accuracy.

When this happens, challenges seem to intensify, because the longer it takes to take action, the harder action becomes. So we complain about how difficult life is, how the problems continue to rise, and how every day it's tougher than the day before. The bad news is, when you defer what's important to deal with what's unimportant, you end up paying a large penalty in the future.

Why We Don't Take Action

Ralph Waldo Emerson once said, "Of what use to make heroic vows of amendment, if the same old law-breaker is to keep them?" I believe he meant we make vows, but we don't do what we know we should and wind up breaking them over and over again due to our failure to take action.

Most of the time, we don't take action because we don't have faith in ourselves or our own ability to deal with the hurdles and adversities that arise as we progress toward where we want to be. We also want to get others involved first. We want people to believe in our dreams and goals and agree with what we want to do, and sometimes if we can't gather up people and get a team together behind our ideas, what we desire becomes undesirable because we're concerned that we will be alone on our journey. We don't realize that as we take action, the people we need will come along at the time we need them. All the knowledge we need will come to us from external and internal sources only at the time we make a move toward our dreams. If we sit still and do nothing, we will never discover what we are capable of truly doing.

We don't have to wait for things to be what we think they should be before we act. Everything does not have to be in place or just right before we can move forward. We can take action even if we aren't in the best position in our lives or our environments aren't what we want them to be. We can't wait for the change to happen before we act; we have to change everything with our actions if we're ever going to alter our circumstances.

Talking about it won't get it done. We don't need to know all of the details to make a move. Gathering all the facts about how things will work out is just another way to procrastinate. Whenever we're going after something that we really want to accomplish, it's not until we're actually doing it that we get an inner core belief that we can push harder. It's not that we can't accomplish the things we want, we just never become aware that we can, because we don't take action. The only thing that's necessary to take the first step is the awareness that you can accomplish the thing that you desire.

Why Not Acting Hurts Our Futures

When we don't act on something right away, it's defined as procrastination. Ironically, we know how it's defined, but still find ourselves caught up in it. After we've procrastinated for a while, we're met with our diminishing intentions. Because we didn't act right away, we begin to make small adjustments in what we want to accomplish, because the inspiration to reach our goal has left us.

Procrastination is one of the biggest barriers to tapping into our power and getting what we want, because it makes us think that somehow tomorrow or next week or next year will be a better time to start. It kills any ambition and causes indecision. If we paid for procrastinating by getting sick right away or immediately losing everything we had, we wouldn't procrastinate anymore. We'd see that procrastination hurts and just costs too much, but procrastination is charming and smooth. It gets you comfortable while luring you in, and then makes you pay years down the line with compounded interest in the form of regret, blame, and an unfulfilled life.

Procrastination says, "You don't have to go after your dreams, build the life you want, or decide today." It tells you to do what you want and be comfortable now, because later it will be better and easier. Unfortunately, we can't foresee the consequences of the smallest things that we fail to do daily, and by the time we realize how difficult things have become and how much time we've wasted, it's too late.

We'll never find our dreams by loose, casual drifting. We all have two natures. One wants us to move forward, be progressive and be all we can in life, while the other wants us to drift through life and quit at every sign of adversity. We must choose not to be influenced by our circumstances instead of becoming the creator of them. Not taking action immediately places us in the position of not really feeling like doing what we've intended to do. The problem is, we don't understand that we're stopping good things from happening in the future by not acting in the present. Every time we delay up front, we suffer the delay of the reward in the future. We don't know what we're missing out on until the compound effect of not taking action hits us, and by then it's usually a disaster. We can't measure the consequences of not taking action right away, because we don't know what the price of delay is immediately. It's the years of inaction that brings about all the results we don't want to experience.

We each have a definite purpose in life, but many of us never discover what it is because we fail to take action. We talk about all the things we want, but when the moment arises, we make excuses instead of seeing the opportunity that's right in front of us due to our poor perception. Our prayers are not answered according to the faith we have while we're talking, but instead according to the faith we have while we're working. No one knows the inner workings of the process, but we spend the majority of our time trying to figure them out. When we can't wrap our minds around how things will work out, we abort the process.

Most of our struggle comes from putting off taking action. Sometimes we want to see how all things will work out before we make a move. Sometimes we know how to get to our dreams, but we don't take action because we don't want to go through hardship and struggle to get there and look for another course. When we delay and sit around wishing good things would happen or waiting for an answer to magically appear, our troubles begin to pile up on us. So many people feel like they can't achieve their goals because there are just too many things in the way. Think about the mother who decides to put all of her dreams on hold to raise the kids, then when the kids are older and have moved on with life, she feels empty because she's neglected her own needs for so many years. Many people find themselves in situations they don't want to be in because they made a decision to act in response to life's circumstances instead of fighting to create the life of their dreams. The fact is, we'll never really know how powerful we are or what we can do until we act.

Your Power to Get What You Want

If there's something we want to accomplish, even if it's small, and we don't take immediate action, we've failed as far as that dream or the thing we wanted to accomplish is concerned. No one will wake you up every morning and ask you how close you are to achieving your dream. No one will hold you accountable for your inefficiency, but there is a life you will reap for the compounding inefficient days you sow.

Life doesn't require anyone to succeed, take action, or achieve their goals and dreams. That's a requirement you must place on yourself. We determine the quality of the life we live by our cause in life, and the effects follow. If we don't want to live a mediocre, undesirable, unfulfilling life, we need to decide first what type of life we want to live.

Creating a clear picture is a good way to start. When we don't have a clear picture or a clear design of the thing we want to go after, we go for and do anything. We end up bargaining with life just to get by, looking for handouts, suffering from a victim mentality and getting beat by a job and a career we really don't want. We make bad decisions, fear going after our dreams, and are afraid of what people may say. When these things happen, we think that they are caused by heredity, karma, or thousands of other external things. We drift along aimlessly unconscious of our power, and we fall right into negative outside circumstances believing there is nothing more to life. And we fail.

You're not restricted from achieving anything you truly desire, no matter where you are, what has happened, what you're going through, or who your family may be. There's no such thing as inheriting a fixed life. Nobody inherits that. We become what we think about, so what our lives become is up to us. When we become conscious of the powers we possess, we can throw away self-imposed limitations and unbelief and think solely about what we want to be.

We all have godlike powers lying dormant inside of us that are dying to be awakened. These powers allow us to be the architect of the lives we desire, the builder with the tools to construct what we want, and to have and be all we can imagine. Instead of identifying and using the power within us, we look to and focus on things outside of us and substitute it with temporary fixes. Instead of doing the things required to get to our goals and dreams, like deciding what we want, learning all we need to know, and going after it, we normally do what is comfortable because it's easy. In the long term, doing that creates lives we don't want. As a result, we charge our way through an undefined, unfocused, and unfulfilling life completely unaware of our power. We blindly walk into turmoil and struggle in uncertainty. Because of this, our daily grind has no major purpose, definite aim, or objective. Instead, we eat, work, sleep, and plow through existence while all of nature and all of life calls upon us to tap into the godlike creative powers we possess. This is surely not the purpose of our existence.

Time for Some Action

After we get through all the blame, excuses, and reasons why we're not moving forward, we have to face ourselves and say, "It's time for some action." I'm not referring to hasty action that has you all over the place or emergency action because something is wrong. I am talking about practicing a few simple disciplines every day to get to your goal.

Today, let go of what could have been and become determined to no longer focus on the past, because there is nothing more that can come from what did or did not happen. We can't act in the future, because the future is not here yet—although the things we do today will affect it. What we can do is act where we are in the moment with our future goal in mind. We can't skip this part of the process. If we are ever going to get the things we want, we must act now, wherever we are and with whatever we have. We have to focus on the joy of advancing toward our dreams today. Many people are so focused on what they are now instead of the new person they'll become that they think they can skip the level they are on. Most of us are rushing to accomplish things because we feel like at our age we should be further along or because we didn't do something by a certain time. We feel we need to speed up the process to get some form of recognition or applause from people. But we can't get to the next level of life until we handle the one we're on right now. Take some type of action right now wherever you are, but don't rush. Focus on the journey and the person you are becoming in the process.

Here are some things you can do to tackle what you're dealing with, get focused, and take action:

Keep Your Goal in Mind

Stop separating the things you think about from the action it takes to achieve them. Remember that you can take action towards success every day and that the accumulation of successful actions over time will ultimately take you where you want to be.

Want It Badly Enough to Do It

Sometimes we simply don't want the change we need badly enough, so we don't take action. When your desire outweighs what's holding you back, you'll pick up steam and move closer to what you want.

Create the Circumstances

Remember that you can create the things that you want by taking targeted and decisive action. George Bernard Shaw once said, "People are always blaming their circumstances for what they are. I don't believe in circumstances. The people who get on in this world are the people who get up and look for the circumstances they want, and if they can't find them, make them."

Don't Neglect the Small Things

A few simple disciplines repeated every day equals success. You don't have to do something grand right away. Just take a small step in the direction of your dreams. Take a small action toward your goal and be efficient. Your days of efficient activity, even though small, will compound until your dream becomes a reality.

Don't Rush Blindly into Things

Many of us are trying to achieve all that we want at one time. When we sit down to eat, we don't shove all the food in our mouths at once. We eat one bite at a time. Remember, it's not the number of things you do, it is the effectiveness in what you do. The moment we take action, even in the smallest form, there is movement. Use these tips to gain momentum:

- Develop a success routine that includes things that you can stick to accomplishing daily. Ask yourself what you can do every day that will help you achieve your goal, and when you find the answer, get to work. Follow the advice of Aristotle, and make excellence a habit.

- Believe you will succeed. If you have an idea or dream, go after it. The main reason we don't achieve what we want is because we don't believe we can.

- Develop a new image of what your life will look like and think of it as a puzzle. Everything you want represents one piece of the puzzle, and as you achieve them one by one, you'll eventually form your whole picture.

- Get around people who take action toward their goals. Most of us spend the majority of time with people who take us away from our goals and not toward them. Get with people that help take you toward your dreams and not away from them.

- Build a motivation bubble. Place pictures of your dreams, blueprints, books, motivations and affirmations around you. Build an atmosphere of achievement by properly conditioning your mind to take action toward what you want.

- Don't let a day go by without taking some type of action toward your goals.

CHAPTER 5

See What You Wish to See

If one advances confidently in the direction of his dreams, and endeavors to live the life which he has imagined, he will meet with a success unexpected in common hours.

– Henry David Thoreau

False Belief

There's an interesting legend from the Middle Ages where a man is arrested and taken down into a dungeon at the bottom of a castle. He's dragged down dark stairs by a big ferocious-looking jailer and thrown into a pitch-black cell. Each day the door opens, a pitcher of water and a loaf of bread are thrown in, and the door is closed again. After twenty years, the prisoner can't stand it any longer. He wants to die, but he doesn't want to commit suicide, so he decides to attack the jailer in hopes that he'll be killed in self-defense and his misery will be put to an end. He examines the cell door carefully so he will be ready when the jailer returns. He grabs the handle, turns it, and to his surprise the door opens. The door wasn't locked, and it never had been. The man gropes along the dark corridor and feels his way up the stairs. At the top, he sees two soldiers chatting. They make no attempt to stop him.

He crosses a great yard without attracting any attention. There is an armed guard on the drawbridge at the gate, but he pays no attention, and the prisoner walks out a free man. The prisoner was a captive not of stone and iron but of a false belief. He was not locked in; he only thought he was. He could have opened the door to freedom at any time if he had changed how he saw his circumstances.

Are you trapped in a prison created by your own way of thinking because you haven't realized that you could be free at any moment? We've all lived in some kind of mental prison, and many of us are still living there every day. Some may be trapped in the prison of fear or guilt while others live in prisons of anger, remorse, pity, and maybe even embarrassment because their lives haven't turned out the way they imagined. This happens when we find ourselves accepting the testimony of our five senses as reality. Our senses bring us an avalanche of sounds, sights, feelings, and concepts that are mostly negative. When we become negative or fearful based on what we see, we attract those conditions. This stems from the false conclusion that we make concerning what we see and the poor decisions we make based upon it.

What holds us back is not in the circumstances themselves but in the image we have of ourselves in the midst of them. Our eyes deceive us and misrepresent the true state of our existence because they only deal with the surface appearance or facts. In reality, we see nothing, because what we see is influenced by what we believe. Shakespeare said, "…there is nothing either good nor bad, but thinking makes it so." In other words, our perception of what we see determines if something is good or bad. This is why we can't judge according to appearances. We must see with our minds, with our eyes closed, because it is there that our vision is spiritual, eternal, and indestructible. We must be positive and poised within. The man who was thrown into prison believed something that was not true, and because his eyes were geared toward what he believed, his eyes deceived him. He thought he was trapped and unable to live the life he wanted to live for twenty years. He had a false image of himself as a prisoner, and so he lived out what he saw.

Destroying False Images

If you're dealing with a false image of who you are, you're not alone. Many of us have that same false image. We feel we're not smart enough, strong enough, attractive enough, or successful enough. We believe we're not fit to take on life's tests. We believe we're failures based on what we see, and because of that, we respond to life that way and encounter situations that are in agreement with our low estimation of ourselves. These events happen to us because we attract them based on the image we have of ourselves.

We have, through the limits we've placed on ourselves, unconsciously created lives we don't want. The good news is you're not stuck. You don't have to stay here. You can destroy any false image you may have of yourself by experiencing what it would feel like to achieve your goals in your imagination. It's called assuming the feeling of your wish fulfilled. By clearly seeing what you want to see, you can change yourself into what you like, but first, you must get rid of the negative image you have of yourself. Forming a new image of yourself as what you want to be at your highest possible self will be a challenge. It requires you to change what you see about you and keep it changed. In order to do that, you must know that you're not a victim of the past or even your present. You can reject that. It does not matter where you are at the moment or what has happened to you. Change this moment, see yourself for the better, and you will change your destiny. At any time, you can see peace in discord, joy in sadness, love in hate, and light in darkness. See yourself doing all those things and being everything that you envision yourself to be. Feel it, see it, and touch it in your mind. It doesn't matter whether you are young or old or rich or poor, it's never too late. The time is now.

The False Image Chain

In Africa, they let baby elephants play all day. Then, at the end of the day, they tie them to a three-foot chain connected to a wooden stake in the ground. When the elephants try to run with the chain on, they get pulled back. Eventually, they become conditioned to only going three feet. The practice is continued until the elephants reach adulthood. It's been said that when elephants become adults, they're strong enough to pull a train car filled with people. But because they've been tethered to a three-foot chain from youth, the only thing that would cause them to rip the chain out of the ground and run is a fire. They don't realize how powerful they are and remain bound.

Today I want you to think about what the chain of having a limited imagination has done to you and how it has kept you bound. I want you to think about all the time you've spent not going after the things you want because of the chain others placed on you—or you placed on yourself. I want you to ask yourself what you've allowed to bind you that you have the power to break free of, and what you are conditioning yourself to believe that is keeping you in bondage. Ask yourself, "Why do I have to wait to see my life on fire before I break free?" What will it take? What age are you willing to wait to reach before you finally gain your freedom?

Whatever the chain is, the thing you see, this is just a picture, it's a movie. If you don't want to look at that picture or movie anymore, you don't have to, but you do need to replace it with a picture or movie you want to see. If you don't imagine what you wish to see, you will always be bound by what you do see.

The Seed

One day, while working with a group of sales professionals in the exercise of image creation, I asked them to create an image of what they wanted in their lives. I gave the group about ten minutes to complete the assignment. As I roamed the room, I noticed that one lady seemed like she wasn't interested in doing the exercise. I stopped and asked her if everything was okay. She nodded yes, but her paper was blank and she stared off, seeming confused. When the group finished the exercise, I asked her about the image she'd created, and a tear fell from her eye. When I asked her what was wrong, she burst out in tears and said, "I don't have an image of the person I want to become."

"Well, if you don't mind me asking, how old are you?" I asked.

"I'm seventy," she replied.

She had lived up to the age of seventy without an image of something worthwhile to go after, and when asked the question, the only thing she could do is think of all the things she hadn't done. For years, she had failed to plant the seed of what she wanted. Life took her by storm, she said, and at that point in her life she was only experiencing what she imagined but not imagining what she wanted.

Napoleon Hill once said, "Whatever the mind can conceive and believe, it can achieve." In other words, you can literally manifest anything you want in life, but to do so you have to first conceive it—have the image of what you want—in your imagination. This means you have to plant the positive things you wish to see in your life in your mind to reap a harvest, but first you need a seed. The seed is the goal, dream, or concept of the thing you truly desire. To plant the seed, we must believe there's no shortage of the number of things we can do or be. There is no lack.

If self-imposed limits are the seeds you've been planting, you will have a harvest, but it will be a harvest of limitation in every area of your life. When we have a limited image of ourselves, it makes us aim low for one of two reasons: it's either all we feel we can achieve, or someone suggested aiming low was okay, and we believed them.

When we understand that we can only attract that which we want in accordance with the measure of our understanding, we no longer go to the ocean of life with a teaspoon. We bring our buckets instead. When we lack understanding, we plant small seeds and get small returns, and most of that stems from the undersized images, dreams, and goals. You must start with a clear and positive seed image and a definite target, but you can't stop there. Your seed must be backed by purpose, and you must constantly visualize what you wish to see and have faith that it's already yours.

The Steady Image

Most of us have no problem seeing the things we want or imagining how life would be if we had them. The problem is we can't visualize long enough, we forget about what we want, and we revert to our old negative images when we are met with what we perceive to be stronger negative circumstances. If you were to take a magnifying glass and reflect sunlight from it onto a piece of paper, the paper will burn because the sun's energy is concentrated into a tiny beam. That's how we have to focus our vision on the things we want. We have to hold tight in concentration until what we want manifests no matter how our circumstances change. We bring into our lives what we concentrate on. You must change your thoughts and keep them changed not for a moment, not for a day or week, but steadily and permanently.

Can you do an exercise with me? For ten minutes, I want you to only think about good, positive, constructive things. You may be thinking, "Come on. You have no idea what I'm thinking about right now," but I want you to give this a try. Can you do that? Great. Think about what you'd want to see happen to you if there were no limitations. If you're dealing with sickness, see health; if you're in a financial dilemma, see what you would do if that was no longer a problem. If you feel stuck somewhere, see yourself free. Just ten minutes, close your eyes. Let's go.

I'm sure in those ten minutes there were a lot of things that crossed your mind. You may even have had some distractions along the way. Were you able to get back to your positive and constructive thoughts despite them? Here's why I challenged you. Most of us can't hold positive images steady in our minds long enough to bring them to pass. When life gets complicated, the positive images we attempt to create get conquered by the negative ones. It's at this point we begin to give birth to all of the negative things we don't want in our lives. Why is that? Well, by our conditioning. We are conditioned to see and imagine the negative, so when we do imagine something positive, it's only for a short period of time. We can overcome this by training ourselves to choose what we think about. Just like with physical exercise, we have to build our mental strength in this area as well. Yes, we all go through challenges in life, but it's important to be conscious of what we're conceiving in the process. If we could not choose the images we have in our minds, we would have no real control over our lives at all. Ask yourself, what images am I conceiving with the thoughts I have while I am going through challenges? When difficulties pop up, do I immediately imagine everything bad that can happen, or do I realize that I have taken my eyes off of what I've imagined for my life?

The things we want don't materialize when our image is of doubt. By the time we realize the harm our doubts can do, we're buried in what we've manifested, all because we believed things like:

- "I can't do it."
- "I can't have it."
- "I can't become it."
- "I can't achieve it."

That's all any of us needs to stop the forward progress to our dreams. Whatever images you have in your mind can take you from where you are to where you want to be. They can also take you from where you want to be back to where you are now if you allow negative images to stay in your mind. Your mind is where all your thoughts, desires, and dreams come from. It's the hub of creation. It allows you to springboard yourself to the life you want to live. Our ability to conceive the right things allows us to create the life we desire and turn ourselves into the person we imagine we can be.

Clear Your Mental Runway

I was on a plane recently when I realized that no matter what goes on, the plane will not move if the runway is crowded. Everything needs to be clear before liftoff. As we were heading to the runway, the plane slowed down and stopped. The captain got on the microphone and said that he couldn't move because the runway wasn't clear. When I looked out of the window, I didn't see anything on the runway, and neither did anyone else, but we were looking from the sides of the plane and not the front. Sensing the passengers were a little nervous, the captain got back on and announced that he couldn't move the plane because there was a family of ducks crossing in front of us. Everything had to stop until they got to the other side.

I looked around, and as I glanced at everyone on the plane, something dawned on me. Everyone was going somewhere in life. Maybe some passengers were starting over in a new place, while others were going on vacation, returning home, or going to work. It didn't matter where they were going, though, because the runway needed to be clear before we could take off.

This is similar to the way our minds work and how our bodies move. Our minds have to be clear for us to have a mental image of our destination. I mean clear of everything, even little things as cute as ducklings that we think won't affect us. We won't be able to imagine the life we want to live with so much junk in our heads from past failures, hurts, and disappointments. I know it may seem difficult to just sit down and move things out of the way mentally, but it's the first step you must take to create a new image.

Ralph Waldo Emerson once said, "A man is what he thinks about all day long." That's why we need to have a clear idea of who we want to be and what we want to achieve. We must have the image of what we want so we can paint the picture we wish to see. Our minds can imagine incredible things beyond our wildest dreams, but sometimes we can fall short of reaching them. We only fall short because the wings of our imaginations are untrained, and instead of flying, we come crashing down, never to get up again. Decide today what you want to see. If you can't see the image of what you want in your mind, you'll never have it in your possession. Deciding what you want is the ignition switch. Creating the image starts the fire.

Live and Act with Conviction

James Allen once said that men are always anxious to improve their circumstances but are unwilling to improve themselves; therefore, they remain bound. If you want to be free of all the things that have held you back, you have to believe that what you imagine is already yours and act with conviction. Don't worry about how everything will play out. Your job is to focus on what you imagine until it becomes a reality.

Knowing what you want is the start of achieving great things, but it's our imagination that gets us there. When we were kids, we imagined being, having, or doing whatever we wanted, and the possibilities were endless. We spent years thinking of one day doing whatever we set our minds to. As time progressed and we grew older, time spent in our imaginations was slowly replaced with real-life issues. Today, let's get back on the path of creating what we wish to see with our imagination.

Here are some important things to remember about the power of your imagination:

1. Your imagination is the gateway to the path you'll venture on to get the life you want.
2. Make sure you are seeing what you want to see. This will ensure you're on the right path.

3. If your imagination and your actions toward what you imagine
    are good, you will never produce bad results.

Whenever we alter our thinking toward what we see, the things we
want alter toward us.

What we imagine is never kept a secret. It crystallizes into our
habits, and our habits become our circumstances. We will never be
able to imagine the large things in life until we develop the ability
to imagine the smaller things. Noted author and founder of *Success*
magazine Orison Swett Marden once said, "The majority of failures
in life are simply the victims of their mental defeats. Their conviction
that they cannot succeed as others do robs them of that drive and
determination which self-confidence imparts, and they don't even half
try to succeed."

Determine today not to be bogged down by what you see. Instead
create what you want to see and believe it to be.

Practice the following exercises to evaluate how you see yourself
and your circumstances:

1. Have you placed yourself in a tiny prison based on what you
    perceive your life to be? Choose three things you can start to
    look at positively today.
2. Very few people are aware that the conditions they have in
    their lives are created by the dominating images they hold of
    themselves. Today, stop thinking of what's wrong and focus on
    what's right. List three things that are going right in your life.
3. Visualize where you want to be, who you want to be, and
    the things you want to accomplish. Be sure not to focus on
    how you'll get the things you want. Make the commitment to

visualize the things you want every morning for ten minutes for the next seven days.

4. Most of the time, we can't create a new image of ourselves because we are preoccupied with what we see instead of what could be. What do you wish to see in your life regardless of what you are looking at now?

5. What little ducks do you need to clear from your runway in order for you to take flight?

CHAPTER 6

Believe in Yourself

You are where you are because of what you are,
and you are what you are because of what you
constantly believe.

– Unknown

The Limited Belief

If you've stopped believing in your dream, why? What made you stop? Did you lose faith? Did it become too challenging? Did someone sell you on the idea that your dream wouldn't work? If so, who? Many times, we stay trapped where we don't want to be because the people around us tell us we're crazy for having big dreams. They say, "Don't you realize that you're doing too much?" and "Good luck with that idea," or "I don't see how that's going to work." What they have are limited beliefs, and they plant defective seeds in our minds. People have a way of forcing their limited ideas and thinking on others because they don't have a vision for themselves. They've never been pushed to go beyond what they know. Being comfortable where they are is their concept of what life is, and they want to make you comfortable where you are there with them by any means necessary. The trouble in most cases is the people who do this don't know they are negative. They talk like they have all the facts on why you shouldn't move forward and like they know all the things that could go wrong. We often accept their negative suggestions without realizing it, but we don't have to. No, YOU don't have the mathematical or scientific facts as to whether you can achieve your dreams or not, but that's not the point. The point is you shouldn't limit what you believe about what you can do because of other people's negative beliefs. Someone's negative concepts about you or life do not have to be your reality.

The science of aerodynamics states that the bumblebee cannot fly because its wingspan is too short and its weight too heavy. But the bumblebee doesn't know what's in the textbook, so it goes ahead and it flies. Why? Because regardless of what it looks like, it believes. So, when someone says what can't be done, the person with faith mixed with a strong belief system says, "I'm going to do it." It can be done regardless of the weight of what has been said, or what other people's negative beliefs are.

The Power of Belief

Belief can pull us toward our futures, but in most cases, our beliefs keep us stuck in the past. The trauma of yesterday, regret, fear of uncertainty, or false beliefs can hold us hostage.

Unfortunately, we can't go beyond what we believe. If we don't want negative outcomes, we cannot hold negative beliefs about ourselves. If you are going to be more than what you are now, you have to stop judging yourself by what you've done and begin to judge yourself in terms of what you will do. You have to let go of the limitations that cause you to feel like there's no benefit in having great expectations, thinking big, or taking action. If we don't believe in something great for ourselves, it doesn't matter what we or others think, say, or do. Our results will be frustration and unhappiness.

Belief is choosing to trust in one thing instead of the other. It's trusting that what you want to happen is already done for you. It's you feeling like you have it now before it manifests in the material world. When you strongly believe, nothing holds you back, and mediocrity, bad health issues, or any other miserable condition won't hinder you. When you believe, you're never a victim of circumstances, because you realize that you only become a victim when you believe you are. No matter what happens, you can always get back on track, because your thoughts and beliefs create the results.

We must believe that there is greatness within each of us waiting to be brought forth. While everyone is destined to become something worthwhile, most of us never get the chance to achieve it. Often, it's because what we are thinking about is limited to where we are in life. In other cases, it's because it just didn't dawn on us that we can really achieve our goals, so we don't try.

You must continue your journey with faith by holding on to the things you truly believe for you—not for anyone else. When people tell you that you don't have the right idea, say you dream too much, the sickness is permanent or tell you to quit while you're ahead, let them keep on talking and you keep on believing in your truth. When what we believe in seems contrary to what we want, things will happen that have nothing to do with the good results we desire. When this happens, the life you truly want to live can only be attained by constantly thinking great thoughts about what you can achieve and believing that there is more out there for you than what you have now.

I want you to know that you are not barred from achieving dreams. You are not incapable of accomplishing what you believe you can. At the lowest points in our lives, while we are staring at what we perceive as our worst, we can climb our way to where we want to be with our beliefs. How do we do that? We start by having a dream and believing that we can make it real.

Earl Nightingale once said that success is the progressive realization of a worthy ideal. Having an ideal will require you to grow. Growing means that you can no longer believe the limiting things that people have said about you or the negative things you've thought about yourself. Most of the time, we only talk about an ideal world or an ideal situation because we don't want to be where we are now. When you say "My ideal home is ..." or "In a perfect world my life would be like ..." or "The thing I really want to do is ...," what you are saying is that you wish your life to be one thing but that the results you've gotten based upon your beliefs show you've settled for the complete opposite. A strong ideal that you hold on to, no matter what's going on in your life or how challenging things may seem, is the bridge from where you are to where you want to be. Strive to reach it. Having an ideal will pull you to your greatness.

Up until now, you may have formed the habit of believing being off-course and pulled away from greatness is okay. This may be in part because you believe yourself to be less than great, as many people do. Maybe you feel like an average person with limited abilities or like a flat-out failure. Some days you may believe you can achieve something and others not so much. Whatever you habitually believe you are, you become. And because of this, you will take yourself to a destination of your choosing or to an unintended location far away from your hopes and plans.

In a recent meeting, one of my clients said, "I'm not where I used to be, but I'm not where I want to be." After thinking about what she said for a moment, I told her, "No, you are not where you used to be, but you are on the way to where you want to be." Why did I say that? Many times, that's how we look at things. No, we are not where we used to be, and that's great, but if we're not grateful for where we are at the moment and for all of its opportunities to grow, become better, and develop, we will never get to where we want to be.

What's the Real Struggle?

"I've had a great deal of trouble in my life, but most of it never happened," is what the majority of people would say if you had an in-depth conversation with them on their deathbeds. Nearly everyone can look back at some point, in most cases not that far back, and say, "If I had only taken that chance," or "If I could do things again, I'd take a different route. I'd be much better off now." I'm sure many of us can admit we've worried about things that have never even happened. We can also confess that the time we spent in unbelief caused a huge delay in us ever getting started on achieving our goals.

The years of struggle to find our true purpose or the failure to realize we have one keeps us locked in a tiny prison of unbelief. We've all thought about what it would be like if we achieved our goals, but we often lack the confidence or courage to get started. We just don't believe. All too often, we don't realize our value or uniqueness, so we become discouraged, which holds us back and takes us off course.

When it looks like there's such a long road ahead of us to get to the life we're believing for, it's easy to think, "Oh, well. What's the use." But this is the point where the road that gets us to our goals begins.

Yes, there is and there will always be struggle, but the struggle is you merely wrestling with your journey. We have to know this, and not get comfortable with the idea that life is just a struggle for existence. Yes, we need difficulties to overcome, mountains to climb, bridges to cross, and walls to stand in front of. But it's here where our belief in who we are allows us to overcome those obstacles. If you are ever going to get to where you believe you should be, you have to believe that you can take possession of your internal world and generate faith, enthusiasm, courage, and confidence. When you understand this, you can envision what you want and make it real. This is the point where our struggles help us uncover who we are and, in some cases, show us that where we are is not where we are supposed to stay. If we truly believe this, it will help guide us to what we really want. If you ask anyone who has achieved any type of success, they'll tell you how narrow the chasm is that separates failure from greatness and how it can be bridged by perseverance and faith—in short, believing in yourself.

The Butterfly Effect

There is a very interesting story about a Guru and a little boy. The boy is intrigued by the process of the caterpillar transforming into a butterfly, so the Guru gives the little boy a cocoon on one condition. He tells the boy the cocoon will start to shake and rattle soon, and he warns him not to do anything to assist the butterfly. The little boy agrees. A few days later when the cocoon starts shaking, the little boy tries his best to ignore it, but when it starts to rattle, he starts to worry. He picks up the cocoon, and as he does, he sees the butterfly's wings struggling to get out. He believes the insect is trapped. He remembers what the Guru said, but feels so bad about the butterfly's condition that he decides to help. He opens the cocoon just enough so the butterfly can get out.

The butterfly shoots out and flies around, and within seconds goes crashing to the ground. Sad, the boy picks up the dead butterfly and goes to the Guru.

The boy says, "I don't know what happened. He didn't make it."

The Guru looks at the boy and says, "You helped it get out, didn't you?"

At first the boy says no, but when he sees the look in the Guru's eyes, he answers "yes" with tears in his. The Guru tells the boy that by opening the cocoon, he interrupted the process. The butterfly wasn't struggling, but was flapping its wings to strengthen them. He tells the boy that by opening the cocoon, he didn't give the butterfly time to get strong enough to fly.

Have you ever been there before? Wanting an end result so bad that impatience and unbelief caused you to jump in on the process, only to have it all fall apart. Even though the boy knew one day there would be a beautiful butterfly coming out of such a tough process, he became impatient. All he thought about was what he saw, and things didn't look right, so something had to be wrong. Wanting to help the process or speed things up because it does not look like we think it should is natural. When we believe in our dream or the ideas we have about ourselves, our imaginations allow us to see the dream; however, the process is always left covered. If we saw that the process doesn't look like the dream, in most cases we would no longer believe.

The process can seem like a struggle. It can be tough and challenging at some points, and it can be a mess, so we want to help by getting involved. The only thing we need to do is grow into the person that is required to achieve the dream. To achieve anything great in life, there will be a process, and it won't always look like what you want it to at times. But in order for you to manifest the life you want, you have to hold tight to the image and believe with confidence that it will happen.

Be Deliberate About What You Believe In

Many people are waiting for some future event to occur for them to start living their dreams or to begin building the lives they want to live. The truth is, deep down they just don't believe in themselves enough to step up and live. They need everything to be perfect and for everyone to have their backs first before they believe. Here's my advice. Don't wait for a distant unknown future when you think life will somehow be better. Life becomes better when we believe that we have the power to overcome our current circumstances. Start today by believing in you. Don't wait for someone else's opinion for you to change. Believe that you can live a prosperous, healthy, and happy life. Believe that you can achieve your goals even after the setbacks, after the heartaches. Obtaining your dream will require you to believe in yourself one day at a time while doing the things that you can, until your life becomes what you believe it can be. Today, look at where you are and know that you can be more, do more and have more. Start by saying:

- I can have.
- I can do.
- I can be anything that I desire to do, have, and be.
- Although I may not be where I used to be, I'm on the way to where I believe I can be.

Believe, believe, believe. Even though something may be a fact, that does not mean it's a reality. Life responds to what you believe. There are desires within you urging you to do bigger things, be better, and to live well and create the life in the material world that you long for. There's a world out there begging you to give it your all so you can have all that you desire. You have unlimited power, and there is unlimited abundance all about, but you must believe this is true to know how to identify it and put it to use. We all have godlike powers and greatness sleeping inside of us dying to be awakened, and life calls upon us to tap into our unlimited power.

What is this unlimited power? It's the power to use your thoughts to get what you desire, become the person you want to be, and accomplish whatever you're striving to obtain. The power rests with you, but you have to believe in yourself.

Ask yourself the following to better understand how your beliefs have impacted your progress toward your goals:

1. What has stopped you from achieving the things you want to accomplish?
2. What are some limiting beliefs you have about yourself?
3. Take a moment to reflect on your limiting beliefs. How have they hurt or helped you?
4. Now that you know you have to be deliberate about what you believe in, list five things that you will focus on and believe that will help you get to your goals.
5. Write down three positive things that you believe about you.

CHAPTER 7

How to Design Your Future

Change this moment and you change your destiny.

– Dr. Joseph Murphy

The Choice

One day, a young man asked Socrates how he could get wisdom. Socrates responded, "Follow me."

The young man followed Socrates to a river. When they got there, Socrates pushed the young man's head under the water and held it there until he gasped for air uncontrollably. Socrates then released the young man's head.

When the young man was able to breathe again, Socrates asked him, "What did you want most when you were under the water?"

He answered, "I wanted air."

Socrates then told the young man, "When you want wisdom as much as you wanted air when you were immersed in the water, you will receive it."

Like the young man, there will come a time in our lives when we have to make a choice. We'll have to choose what we want for our lives, and we'll have to decide whether we want to do what it's going to take to get it. When we make the decision, everything has a way of flowing into our lives to aid us, but if our vision is limited and we're focused on how our circumstances look presently, the choices we make will be restricted by our lack of vision. The question is, are we willing to fight for it? Are we willing to stake everything we have on the manifestation of our dreams? If our current situation is contrary to what we desire, will we cave in and give up?

The moment we decide what we truly want and go after that goal or become excited for change, life pushes our face in the water just like Socrates did to the young man. Sometimes the obstacles don't come right away, but guess what? They are coming, and they're coming just to see if we really want what we say we do. The obstacles, roadblocks, mountains, and the trials we face will, at times, make it feel like we're suffocating. Our problems can become overpowering when our goal doesn't seem to outweigh the trial. Sometimes, if we're honest, it may feel like we won't survive because our challenges overwhelm us and may seem to deprive us of something we need like air. When this happens, we have to tell ourselves that we're going to choose our dreams no matter what it's going to cost, and we have to tell ourselves that we're willing to fight for what we want.

You have to be willing to choose your dreams over your fears, to choose peace over chaos, and to choose happiness over sadness. In order to do that, you have to believe that your life will be better than what you are facing right now. The feeling of suffocation serves as a necessary reminder. It stirs up the fight inside that's required for you to keep going when your back is up against the wall, or when you're in a tight space, or when things don't seem easy. You have to know that the thing that feels like it's suffocating you is only temporary, and that what you're going through is what it's going to take to get the best out of you.

You have to choose to push forward even though you can't see the finish line and don't know when what you want to happen will happen. When you make the choice and have an intense desire to obtain a goal or to become the person you want to be, there is no obstacle, roadblock, or setback that will stand in your way. When you want something bad enough, you're willing to pay the price for it, and the price you pay is the sacrifice of lesser wants. It's throwing away the unnecessary things, concentrating on the one that's essential, and applying your will to its attainment or accomplishment. Only you can do something about it. Nothing will happen on its own. Life has equipped you with the ability and know-how to create the life of your dreams.

Start Where You Are with What You Have

Oftentimes, people say to me, "I know what I want." Then they ask, "How do I get started?" They say they know they're supposed to do something or be somewhere other than where they are in their lives at the moment, but that they feel stuck. They tell me that they've been through so much, and that their problems have been so overpowering and required more than what they could give that they don't know what to do or where to begin.

I'll tell you what I tell them. The first step lies with you. Many times, we wish we were somewhere other than where we are now. We wish we were doing something different, had a better life, or simply that the limits were removed so we could do everything we wanted. These wishes are important, but having them granted immediately would cause us to skip important steps. First, you must know where you are. To find where it says, "You are here," on your map of life, you must understand the role you played in reaching your present location and come to the realization that if anything is going to get accomplished that will take you to your desired destination, you'll be the one doing it.

Raymond Charles Barker once said, "An unintelligent use of mind can only produce an unintelligent result." That means we can't escape today's poor results if our past decisions were poor. It's choosing to take ownership of what you've created up to this point. It also means taking ownership of where you want to go, and that requires you to clearly and carefully write out the dreams you have and the things you want to change. It's understanding that you are where you're supposed to be at this moment, but what you're doing needs to change for your dreams to become reality. Until you've learned that where you are currently is due to the choices, ideas, goals or lack thereof you've had in the past, you have not taken the first step towards your goal.

Next, set up a routine. Instead of just letting things happen, choose what your mind will focus on daily. You must be laser-focused on who you want to be, where you want to go, and what you want to do, because absolute and disciplined steps are needed to get there.

Many of us have hope, motivation and aspiration, but we don't have a technique to make them come alive. Every great person who has ever achieved the heights of success has done so because they knew where they were, they focused on their goal, and they created a plan or technique that would get them where they wanted to go. Greatness is not inherited. Everyone starts somewhere other than where they want to be, but the difference between those who achieve their goals and those who don't lies in the thoughts, feelings, and actions of the person.

I'm reminded of how trees somehow spring up on rocky ledges or on the sides of mountains where there isn't enough nourishment to even keep moss alive. After the tree's seed is planted, it breaks through its shell and shoots upward. It reaches out and uses all the power it has to spring forth. When it finds it does not have enough energy to sustain itself, it puts forth roots to draw the necessary nutrients from the soil, but soon finds there isn't enough soil on the rocky ledge to give it moisture or nourishment. The one thing the tree does not do is get upset about where it is or what process is needed to get started. It sends its roots into every small space until they reach what it needs to survive, sometimes even splitting giant rocks in search of food. It goes through obstacle after obstacle until it exhausts every food source and gets what it needs. It does all of this because it knows that its purpose in life is to grow, live, and to produce more by living.

Just like the tree, we must go through our own growth process, but in order to do so, we have to find our purpose and know what we want to grow into. This process is not someone else's. No one can do the growing for us. This is the point where we must ask ourselves what our true purpose in life is, what our big goal is, and what our dreams are.

We must understand that what we decide to do when we reach the tough places in life will lead to a result. Indecision leads to a result, waiting leads to a result, confusion leads to a result, and not living your life with meaning every day leads to a result. Many times, we let our dreams slip away because we didn't dig deep enough or push hard enough. Sometimes we've made poor choices. We didn't have clarity at that crucial point in our journey, so we didn't want to go through all the things we needed to go through to be who we thought we wanted to be. Since we didn't realize who we truly were, we ended up where we didn't want to go, and now all that's left for us to do is start over.

Theodore Roosevelt once said, "Do what you can with what you have right where you are." I don't believe he was saying if things are not good for you, do what you can to survive and just continue to live that way. What I do believe he was saying was no matter what's going on at the moment, evaluate yourself by looking at what you do have and finding out who you really are and then building something great from that point. Never mind what you've been through and how you went through it. Focus on where you are and where you want to be.

You can evaluate what you have by asking yourself:

> What talents do I have?
> What skills do I possess?
> What can I do to become a better person?
> What can I do to make a positive contribution to someone or something?
> Who can I forgive?
> What negative ideas about myself can I let go?
> What things from my past can I let go?

Like the seed in the rocky soil, answering these questions may force your nucleus to work harder and dig deeper, but it will also give it vitality enough to draw what it needs from the soil. Change your thoughts, start focusing on what you can do, what you can accomplish today, and who you can be by taking the necessary action and creating a plan to get there.

Change Your View

One of the biggest problems today is too many people lack the ability to look ahead with great expectations and actually believe the things they desire can come to pass. It's normal to view our future as uncertain and, in many cases, potentially disastrous, because we just have so many problems. We dread tomorrow and the week ahead, and we spend our time hurrying to accomplish more and more things that are unimportant. We must understand that we only magnify the negative things we're going through when we spend all of our time worrying and focusing on them. Spending the majority of our time thinking about everything that's going wrong destroys our ability to have a different perspective about ourselves and our lives. It also keeps us from taking action in the right direction. We can't allow our conditions, obstacles, or the trials we're facing to impair our view and ruin our ability to see better for ourselves, because what we believe to be true about ourselves becomes a law of action in our lives. We can create negative patterns by replaying the things we fear and things people have said or by thinking about things like failure and not achieving the same way others have. The minute you change your view about what you give power to, you don't need to remain in that predicament anymore. Life allows you to think as you wish, but it always produces for you what you think about. Changing your view requires you to start thinking differently.

Start by asking yourself a few important questions:

1. What is the first thing I would do if I knew I could have the life I desire?
2. What would I feel if I were living the life of my dreams already?
3. What is the first step I would take to get to my dream?

It's important to keep your view of your future positive no matter what others say or believe and even if you struggle believing. You have to take a personal stand on what you view for you. Changing your view means self-reflection or self-analysis. It's choosing to view things differently while you're in the midst of problems and difficult situations. I will admit, this is going to be a challenge, but it's not impossible. Decide today to drop negative thinking and comparisons. Change your view on what you've blamed yourself for, where you are now, and all of the reasons why you're there. Look at your future with confidence and expectation. Let go of the belief that another person is equipped to determine the quality of your life. You have acknowledged long enough that you've missed the mark in some areas, thought you'd be in a better position, or that you didn't do what was required to reach your goals. Let that go. Holding yourself hostage to something you no longer have control of only hinders your ability to move forward. Look beyond where you are now.

If that seems challenging, especially if there is chaos everywhere, you have not conditioned yourself to see the good, and you are just looking at things with your eyesight. Here's my advice. Close your eyes, use your mindsight, and JUST BEGIN. When you do, you're halfway there. You can take the first step toward achieving your goals and starting where you are with what you have by doing something as simple as changing your perspective.

Try this simple exercise. It can help you create your own personal breakthrough today. Close your eyes and imagine you're in the world that you really want to be in doing everything you have always desired to do. Don't think about anything else. See yourself around the people you want to be around, in the neighborhood you want to live in, and living the life you want for yourself and your family. With your eyes closed, nothing is hindering your vision and you can see clearly through your mind's eye. Now, begin to visualize your current situation from a different point of view. In this new and different view, take action by telling yourself that you're no longer giving time, energy, or effort to the things that you don't want, which are the things you see with your natural eyes. The new world that you've imagined is the world you want to be in. Hold that image until it becomes your reality.

A new perspective helps you see your life and your problems differently. Our thoughts create good or bad things in our lives. The way we were thinking previously created our present circumstances. For us to create the circumstances of happiness, love, joy, health, or freedom, we have to change our perspective and view them differently. You have to think positively about your life, your dreams, and your goals everyday repetitively. This helps you focus on your goals and dreams and keeps your mind off the things you don't want. It motivates you to see only the good things you desire.

What are some things you want in your life right now?

More income?
Better health?
Happiness?
A new job?
Better relationships?
To start a business?

To obtain these things and have a better view of yourself, your thoughts must be equivalent to what you want, not comparable to what you are dealing with. It's important to make the choice to take a new perspective, because the decisions you make today create the life you will inhabit in the next few years and far into the future. We don't just arrive at our desired destination by default, we do so because of the sum total of all of the things we choose to do or not to do daily.

Ask yourself, if you don't change your thinking about what's going on, how can your circumstances and your life change for the better? If you don't seek the answers to these questions, how will you reach a positive solution to your problems? Regardless of your current limitations, struggles, or setbacks, make the choice to see things from a better perspective, ask important questions, and start where you are with what you have.

Do You Have a Blueprint?

Most of the time, our goal seems too far to reach when we make the decision to go for it, and typically our progress appears painful and slow. In most cases, it looks like we won't make it. Sometimes it seems easier to go back to what we were doing before and revert to old habits that feel comfortable but usually lead us where we don't want to be. Well, there is a way to beat this. You need a success blueprint. Think about building a home for you and your family. You'd more than likely be extremely involved in the creation of the blueprint that maps out where you want things in your house. You would make sure the builders are creating exactly what's on the blueprint. You'd spend time visualizing what your home will look like when it's done, and the furniture and your family are there. You would make sure everything was on track. You would be sure to select the highest quality building materials and the best of everything for your home.

Building a successful life is the same way.

Just like a home, everything you do in life requires a blueprint. If your life is filled with worry, anxiety, and fear, you have a blueprint, but it's the wrong one because it doesn't give you a good point of reference for what you're building. A bad blueprint can be the reason your focus is on all the things that have nothing to do with your dreams and why you never seem to get on track. Every day we build a home in our minds. Our thoughts and imagination become the blueprint that we build our lives according to every day. If we are not positive, definite, and clear with where we want to go and with what we are building, our blueprint will not produce the lives we want. Randomly saying, "I want this," or "I want that," and "This is how I think my life should be" without having a way to get there is daydreaming. You need to know what you are building and why. The blueprint is the big picture, the end goal. Get as clear as the captain of a ship sailing toward a port. He may not be able to see it physically, but he doesn't look behind him or to the side to find it. He knows his destination is in front of him.

Many times, we don't have a blueprint because we're focused on two things, where we are and where we don't want to be. You can only end up in one place, so it's important for you to focus solely on your goal. Here is a question I had to answer myself. It's what got my blueprint going.

"What do I want life to look like for my children now and when I am gone?"

If you don't have children, here's an even bigger question: "What do I want the world to look like now and when I am gone?"

You see, when you answer questions such as these, you start to look at the big picture in a new way. You will be able to choose wisely, think differently and understand that every action you take is either taking you to a goal or taking you away from it. When we choose to give our time and energy to things that are not in our blueprint, we are no longer focused on the big picture. This keeps the inlet of our new thoughts and ideas closed and preserves all the things we dislike, which magnifies our problems. The biggest challenge that makes us afraid to build our blueprints is what I call I-can't-itis.

> I can't because I am broke.
> I can't because I am sick.
> I can't because I don't have the ability.
> I can't because there is no opportunity for me.
> I can't because I grew up in a bad environment.
> I can't because I am too young or too old.
> I can't because (fill in the blank).

I-can't-itis destroys our ability to create our blueprint and kills our dreams. You must retain the ability to see that you have unlimited wisdom, guidance, creativity, substance, and supply with which to create a solid blueprint to achieve your goals. You must choose to let go of your self-imposed limitations before you begin. No matter where you are in your life at this very moment, you have to choose to see the future as you want it to be. You have to believe that your life does not have to end in failure or destruction. You have to decide to use the I Can mindset. You have to believe in your big picture. You can begin creating your success blueprint today by choosing fresh ideas for your future. You are the master of your fate, the captain of your soul, and the architect of your life. You have within you the power to build a bright and rewarding future.

The Choice to Weigh Before You Pay

I took a lot of fruit to the counter one day while I was at the grocery store. I chose not to weigh any of it. When I got to the counter, the fruit cost much more than I thought it would, so I had to make a choice. Should I pay because I'm at the counter and there's a line forming behind me, or should I put everything back? I decided there was a possibility that I wouldn't even eat it all, so I put most of it back. Then, I started thinking about my life and how many decisions I've made without actually weighing the cost before paying the consequences.

We've all had to deal with consequences that made us wish we had thought deeply before making a move or saying yes. The things we have chosen to do were all based on our limited understanding of what we would pay, so we made a fingers-crossed choice. When we make too many blind choices, the weight of the consequences can cost us in years.

Relationships: The blind choice of entering a relationship quickly can cost you heavily. Likewise, staying in a bad relationship that impacts you negatively can have you pulling yourself out of years of trouble. Weigh every relationship around you, and if it doesn't help you toward your dreams, it's time to cut the cord.

Business: It's very important to weigh your options so that you can make the proper decision before jumping into any business venture. Seek wise counsel. Be certain to know everything about your field and about the track record of the people you'll be working with. Don't be quick to sign things, and review everything before putting your name on the dotted line.

School: When I was young, I was told to get good grades, graduate, and get a good-paying job. That's the dream. Now, I'm not saying don't go to school. I'm saying to find out what your goals are first, determine if going to school aligns with them, and then weigh your options. There are far too many people in the world that aren't using their degrees or are repaying student loans after earning degrees for things they don't even want to do.

Work: It's been said that we spend one-third of our lives working, and most of the time, it's somewhere we don't want to be. If you plan to work for twenty-five to forty years of your life, be certain it's in a field you choose and adds value to you as much as you do to it.

Failure

It's just as easy to see ourselves as successful as it is to see ourselves as failures, and sometimes we spend so much time weighing all of the things that could go wrong that we end up suffering from years of regret for never taking the first step. When we hold the belief in our minds that some undesirable condition already exists, it keeps us on the sidelines. Many people choose not to go after their dreams because they believe they won't succeed, so the weight of potential failure causes them not to take action. They are scared to try because they don't want to fail. Have you ever been there before? Sometimes, ironically, the weight of failure can outweigh success.

If you don't want to lose or fail, choose to focus on winning. It's been said many times that failure is not an option, and while that sounds nice, the truth is, to be successful at anything you must fail. Success hinges on how you deal with failure, because success is not possible unless you choose to learn from your errors. Failure only leads to success if you choose to get stronger and wiser and decide to expect more from yourself and from life.

Energy

Choosing where you direct your energy can be the difference between burnout and achievement. We have to learn how to place our energy in the things that will move us toward our dreams. It's been said that it took Thomas Edison 9999 times getting the light bulb wrong before getting it right the 10,000th time. He put all his efforts into one thing, and realized his future success would be determined by his concentrated and persistent energy. He had a target, and no matter what was going on, he remained focused.

Decide what you want your life to look like and focus all of your attention on achieving that. Choose to remove your energy from every person, place, and negative idea that is contrary to what you want, and direct your attention to what you want to accomplish. When we don't direct our energy towards a goal, it gets spread out and goes to too many different places. When this happens, we're busy but not achieving anything, and we always seem depleted and tired. Some of the things we do that take us away from our dreams and deplete our energy are:

Spending Too Much Time Looking at Everyone Else

Unfortunately, we often spend so much time stat checking everyone else and what they're doing that we never focus on our own stats. The time we spend thinking about others can be used to look at us and see where we are in our lives. It's much easier to look at others' stats. The challenge lies in keeping the stats on who we are, where we're going, and what we want to accomplish.

Thinking Too Much About Past Failures

Have you ever told yourself secretly, "I know I can do this, but my past failures are blocking me from moving forward?" It's like we have a protective mechanism in us that says, "Hey, wait! You know you failed last time. I don't think this is a good idea to try." So, instead of thinking about whether we can, we're focused on why we can't.

Thinking About What Others May Think

This is sad but true. We spend too much time thinking about what other people think of what we decide to do. We ask, "If I decide to start my own business, go back to school, or quit this dead-end job, what will my family think? What will my friends say?"

What If This Just Does Not Work Out for Me

We tell ourselves, "I've been here before. I know I really want this change, I know it's for the best. But what if I finally do this and it doesn't work?" Far too often, we spend too much time thinking about whether we are making the right decisions because we really don't believe things will work out in our favor.

It's Going to Take Me Too Much Time to Accomplish My Goals

Have you ever said, "This goal is going to take me too long to reach?" We actually don't have a time on when we will achieve our goals, but the longer it takes for us to decide to start, the longer it will take to get what we want.

I Will Wait for Things to Change First Before I Change

In short, this is saying that you'll lose weight first, then go to the gym, that you'll get things first and then be happy, or that you will meet the person of your dreams first and then your life will change. Waiting for change is one of the main reasons we never change. We have to start the process.

I Will Start Tomorrow

Starting tomorrow leads to weeks, years, and decades of never starting. The moment you decide what you want to do, you have to get going immediately. "I'll start tomorrow" eventually becomes "I should have started years ago."

No one else on earth is better equipped to determine what's good for your life than you. To say you don't know what to do or you don't know what you want is to negate the powers within. There are no favorites. There may be some people with more factual knowledge and more experience, but that is only because they made a choice to take action and they directed their energy to the attainment of their goals. They decided to think new ideas, get more information, read more, and execute definite, clear plans based on what they learned. They didn't stay stagnant. They concentrated their energy and took the leap.

When the oyster gets little grains of sand inside of its shell, it gets irritated. It tries its best to get rid of them, but when it discovers it can't, it settles down and stops focusing on the sand. Instead, it sees the benefit and proceeds to use its energy to produce one of the greatest things in the world, a pearl. The oyster could choose to stay frustrated about the sand, but instead it chooses to focus its energy and produce something of value with it. No matter the difficulty, no matter the challenge, the choice is yours to produce something great out of what challenges you. Here is my recommendation. Get to pearling today.

There comes a time in all of our lives when we have to make a difficult choice. Many of us make the easy choice, not realizing that poorly thought-out choices made today may trigger bigger, harder choices that will need to be made in the future. In most cases when the future arrives and things don't turn out the way we thought they would, we figure out that we should have made better choices years ago. Then, we make the poor choice to dwell in the outcome of our bad decisions.

What is the most difficult thing you're facing right now? Tell yourself it's the best thing that could happen, because it's teaching you a lesson that will turn into a pearl that will help you grow and reveal unseen possibilities. Like the oyster, focus your energy on that difficult choice and look at it as an opportunity to create new ideas, new dreams, and new goals. Choose to accept the reality that the difficulties in your life are not permanent. Choose new healthy, positive thoughts, which will ultimately lead to new habits and a new life.

Design vs. Default

A professor at a university once said, "The university pays me for doing what I would happily do for free." Most people may laugh at that idea, but what he was really saying was that his work was not just a place to tediously make a living but an opportunity to joyously live a making. He was designing his life the way he wanted it to be. He allowed his work to give him the opportunity to grow as a person, be creative, and use his talents to the fullest. Living by design is all about creating a blueprint, concentrating your focus, and doing what you choose to do.

If we choose not to design our lives by setting goals that get us to our dreams, our lives will be designed for us by default. Often when that happens, we end up just getting by, working in jobs we hate, living where we don't want to live, driving a car we don't like, and shopping where we can barely afford to shop. This is not the life we want to live. If the things you're doing right now aren't getting you to where you need to be, you can choose to design a different life today. Start by writing down what you want your life to look like. Write down what you want for yourself, where you want to be, and what you want to do and have. Be specific and write it out in the most detailed way. Then, find out everything there is to know about the things you want to accomplish and get to work doing those things in your life.

It's time to take a stand. Every day that you wake up, you have an opportunity to win, but you have to know how to play the game. You start by choosing to bet on yourself. You can only do that when you believe in yourself to the fullest and realize that the only person you need to impress is you. You have to know that you deserve the best, and the best is health, wealth, love, and perfect self-expression in its highest forms. You have to believe that all of the time and effort you will put into what you want to accomplish will allow you to perform at your highest level and accomplish the tasks that will change your life for the better. You have to hold tight to the image of what you want your life to look like, and believe it has no choice but to materialize sooner or later. There is a place in life that no one else can fill but you. There is something you have to do while you are here on Earth that no one else can do. Choose to step up to the plate of life and believe that all of your dreams can be fulfilled. Today, choose to design your future!

Answer these questions to begin designing a better future:

1. What are three decisions that you have to make but keep choosing to put off?
2. To get results, you must know what you are building. Do you have a blueprint for success?

3. Are you weighing the potential outcome of your actions so you don't have to pay the price?

4. What did you choose to do today that seemed more important than working on your dreams?

5. Do you live your life by design, or do you live your life by default? If you live by default, what are some changes you can make today to begin living by design?

CHAPTER 8

Your Meaning for Life

You can have anything in life that you really want, but you must be prepared to take the responsibilities that go with it. God is ready the moment you are.

– Emmet Fox

Get Rid of the Mental Stump

I recently read a story about a horse that became afraid whenever he came to a particular tree stump in the ground. Every time the horse got to this stump, he shied away from it. Realizing there was a problem, the horse's owner took the tree stump out of the ground, burned it, and leveled the ground as well. However, for the next twenty-five years, every time the horse passed the place where the stump had been, he became frightened. The problem was the horse was afraid of the memory of the tree stump. Although it had been gone for a long time, the memory of it caused him to live in a continual state of fear.

Many of us live like the horse. We block our happiness, peace, and joy, with our own thoughts and negative mental imagery. Like the tree stump, the things we feared, memories of being misused and hurt, and the situations we worried about can be dug up and even burned, but we can keep replaying and holding the mental images on the screens of our minds. Many people wait for their feelings to change, but that's not how it works. We have to work the change until the feeling kicks in. Most of the time, we don't feel like doing what we know we should, and that's part of the reason we never get to do it. If we waited for the right feeling, we'd be waiting for a long time.

The moment we realize that we have the power to replace the mental stump by planting action, happiness, faith, success, love, and achievement, we can begin to discover the meaning of our lives. It's as simple as choosing to see your life the way you want it to be and thinking positively about yourself and your ability to achieve your dreams and goals. Good things come to us as a result of our state of mind, and we have the freedom to choose what that is. The moment you get clear about the mental stumps that you've allowed to hold you hostage, you'll realize that you can overcome any circumstance, solve any issue, become who you want, and achieve what you want even beyond your wildest dreams.

That's when desire truly kicks in. Desire waits for something to happen, a trigger. A song or a message we hear may motivate us, or a movie or book may contain all of the answers we're looking for and help us to realize what life can be like for us. Seemingly negative occurrences like a confrontation with a friend or enemy, an unexpected layoff, a sudden breakup, homelessness, the death of a loved one, or flat out disgust can also be triggers that ignite desire. Even these unfortunate events can nudge us to greatness because they often wake us up and put us on the right course.

If you've done some things that you felt in the past were bad, it's important for you to know that you're not an evil person. In fact, no one is evil. You didn't mean to be vicious or lack strength in your past. You were just doing what you could with the stuff you had. If you cringe every time you come to the stumps in your life, you have to stop and realize that you're facing your own reaction. You are simply facing a phase of your life that causes resentment. If you've lived long enough, you've made mistakes and failed at some things. Don't allow disappointments, hurts, and setbacks to continue to steal your happiness. Right this second you can choose to rip up those mental stumps by digging deep, planting good things, and realizing that your life has meaning.

Your Expectation Gauge

If you have been going down the road of not expecting great things for yourself, I want you to know that you do not have to keep traveling in that direction. Take a moment and examine your expectations. What are you currently expecting of yourself, your life, and from the places, things and people around you? Are they low or high? Answering these questions will let you know if you're in a healthy space. Our expectations serve as our mental gauge. They help us to see what we really want from life. In most cases, we're stuck because we don't expect much, and getting over our mental stump is not something we ever expect to really do. Our expectation gauge helps us by indicating what changes need to be made and where in terms of what we expect out of our lives.

I want you to think about where your expectation gauge is. Most of the time, we don't know until we study ourselves and discover that the things we expect are things we don't really want for ourselves, or we find out that we simply may not be expecting much at all and are just coasting. Sometimes, minor setbacks or overthinking makes us numb, and we get stuck worrying about how everything we want is going to happen. If we continue to base our expectations on the mistakes and let-downs of our past or the current limitations we are now facing in life, we will never know that we are only experiencing them because of our misunderstanding or ignorance of them. You have to come to the realization that if you are to discover the true meaning of your life, your expectation has to change in order to allow you to easily rise above your limits.

If this is where you are, it's important to ask yourself why you don't expect the greatest life and future for yourself. Ask yourself why you expect pain, struggle, poverty, and continued guilt because of past mistakes or false ideas. If you're not careful, low expectations will hover over you like a dark cloud, and you'll begin to discover that you are comfortable with them. If we continue to look at life as it is, we will constantly allow life to tackle us, break us, and abuse us, assuming that's what's meant for us. If you've been thinking "It is what it is" and "I will take life as it comes," you are not expecting good for your life, and it's time to change your expectation gauge.

You Are Not Average

Life never stops moving, and it expects you to do the same. You were not born to remain stuck or be average. In fact, no one was. Life was designed so we can grow and expand to our full potential. No matter what anyone has ever said to you or what you may have ever felt about yourself, you were not created to be an average person. Far too many people have the false idea that they cannot live greater than they've been living or that where they want to go is an elusive destination they can't reach, so they don't take action to create the lives they want. If you've hit a wall, are living in fear, or don't think you can't recover from a loss, I want you to know that there is greater for you. This must become your deep-rooted belief if you are to rise above being average. You have to know the more that you want is inside of you. What you believe about you depends on you knowing and taking charge of what is going on in your mind. The people who rise above average living and standards do so because they are always seeking to advance toward greater meaning. They know what they want and use the right concepts and methods to reach it. They never have a closed mind.

Yes, You Are a Diamond in the Rough

In Acres of Diamonds by Russell Conwell, there's a story about an African farmer who hears about other farmers finding diamonds and making millions because of it. The stories motivate him so much that he eventually sells his farm and goes looking for diamonds himself. The farmer spends the rest of his life searching for diamonds, but, unfortunately for him, he never finds any. Weary from searching, he throws himself in a river and drowns.

Meanwhile, one day when the farmer who purchased the land from him crosses a small stream on the property, he sees a sudden bright flash of blue and red light come from the bottom of the water. He reaches down and picks up the rather large stone. Admiring it, he takes it home and puts it on his fireplace but thinks nothing of it.

Weeks later, a visitor comes by, notices the huge stone on the fireplace, picks it up and almost faints. He asks the new farmer if he realizes what he's discovered.

The new farmer says, "No. I assumed it was some crystal."

It turns out that he had found one of the largest diamonds ever discovered. The new farmer told his visitor that there were tons of diamonds in the river of different sizes. Well, the farm that the previous farmer sold so that he could go looking for diamonds turned out to be one of the most productive diamond mines on the entire African continent. The first farmer owned free and clear acres of diamonds that he sold for practically nothing in order to look for them elsewhere.

It's important that before you change your mind about things, move on, or give up on you that you take the time to study who YOU are, what you are dealing with, and what the true meaning of life is for you. Yes, your life has meaning. It's to express your hidden talents and to find your true place in life. It's to experience the joy of contributing to the growth, happiness, and success of yourself as well as others. We must come to the realization that life is meaningful no matter where we are, and despite whatever it is we are going through or have been through. All of us are here to give our talents to the world. The faster we understand this, the sooner we can begin anew and create a different and better ending for ourselves.

Studying yourself allows you to see what you can do and to learn who you truly are. Too often, we quit on ourselves because we overvalue other people and the things they can do and undervalue ourselves. Here's what I want you to know. We are not victims of some horrible past. Whatever we're searching for can be found in our own acres of diamonds right where we are. If you don't know what you are capable of, you'll succumb to negative and difficult conditions every time. When we have a true understanding of the meaning of our lives, we know we have a much larger purpose and that we can achieve our goals. All of us can accomplish things beyond our wildest imaginations, and the future can all be new the minute we decide we want it to and when we choose to quit looking elsewhere for the answers, happiness, peace, and prosperity. As Earl Nightingale once said, "While we are looking at other people's pastures, people are looking at ours."

If we recognize what a diamond looks like in its rough state, we would understand that everything in life has a process. Unfortunately, the first farmer didn't know what a diamond in the rough looked like. He was searching for it as it appears when it's been shaped and polished. Diamonds go through a tough process to look like they do when we finally see them. Similarly, we must be able to identify our raw abilities and to refine them, but we have to be patient with ourselves and with what we are building to discover the riches that we seek for ourselves.

The Ending is the New Beginning

It's easy to fall into the habit of being complacent for years on end without even being aware of it. Responsibilities, commitments, jobs, and family can put us in a dull routine. Complacency usually is the cause. It's a destructive mindset, and when we're in it, we no longer get to see what life has in store for us. The things we truly desire for ourselves we don't accomplish because we become comfortable with things being as they are. It can take months or years before we are aware of the chaos it's produced in our lives. It's almost as if we've been blindfolded and walked to a place that we simply didn't want to be.

We usually only wake up from our complacency coma when a serious situation causes us to re-evaluate where we are. When this happens, we realize that every day for the past x amount of years we were drifting and simply lost ourselves. At this point, some people think they're too old to reach their dreams and experience the joys of life. At middle age, you may have limited goals and continue to drift due to a false sense of security and a belief that change is too hard to do, yet deep down inside there is a nagging feeling that tells you that your life can be greater than it is right now. Ask yourself, what would you do if the things you became so comfortable with were taken away with a snap of the finger and you had to start from scratch.

Let's focus on a new beginning. You can start by taking a deep breath and inhaling and exhaling. This is how simple letting the past go is. The only way to move on is to release what you chose to hold on to, especially if it's not allowing you to move forward. We no longer have to live with a false belief that life has to be some hard fight or a struggle to win, nor do we have to live with the nightmares that we replay over and over. As tough as it may be, when you let go of the past, your ideas, your vision, your dreams, and your destiny changes. You may be holding on to things that have run their course or to people who no longer belong in your life, but by changing your outlook and beliefs about your future at this moment, your future becomes something that you can look forward to. Life only becomes a struggle when we're not clear about what we want our future to be and when we don't have a target or goal to achieve.

Decide today on a new and fresh situation or condition that you want right now in your life. Be definite in this decision. Do not limit your decisions by investigating the reasons why it won't happen. If you do, you'll take a detour that will lead you on the path right back to where you are. All false ideas have to be ruled out of your mind. If they get a small ounce of light, even for a moment, what you decide for your future will be robbed of its authority, and you won't act on it. Ask yourself if your decisions today will be based on today's experiences guided by the wisdom you've gained from the past, or will they be determined by old patterns? If you choose the latter, you'll continue to have bad outcomes.

To create a new beginning, you have to no longer fear the future. You have to plan it with excitement. It all starts with you understanding the meaning of your life and your present way of thinking. What you desire in your heart is your greatest asset. It proves that what you want, you can have when you make your mind up to have it, but it needs your attention. What you want should never be pushed to the side, ignored, or forgotten. People die with unfinished business and unfulfilled desires because they never acted on them. They were too consumed with life, too busy, lazy, or tired.

If a ship is traveling at its highest speed but going the wrong way, it has to slow down before it heads in a new direction. Having new thoughts is just the same way. New thought habits won't change your destination overnight, but having them means that your direction will begin to change. It means that you've chosen to have a different outlook, and that allows a positive flow to come into your life and that you've stopped giving energy to the things you don't want. Every moment of the day, we have the opportunity to choose which direction we want to go. However, we skip checking up on our thinking and feelings and breeze into ports and destinations we never choose. If we are going to get to begin anew, we cannot be weighed down by past ideas, past setbacks or challenges. They will not fit in the new life we want to build. It's odd that in today's world we keep our phones, fashion, and a list of other things up to date, but we don't keep our thinking up to date. Your thoughts about you will show you where you are. Do you say yes to the things that inspire you? Do you do things that help you grow? Do you continually search out ways to be better and do more?

New thinking creates new circumstances. Our ideas about ourselves should be concentrated, and our purpose should be what we devote ourselves to daily until it materializes.

When we begin to live and work with great purpose, we get into the flow of great forces, and we attract great minds and great souls. The greater the idea that you are working for, the greater your work will be, and when your work is great you become a great power for good for others and for yourself. Your life is in your hands. You can live it as you wish and you can have whatever you desire, because there is no limit to life and no limit on your capacity to live. So get a new idea about you. Go after that dream, that goal, or that ideal. Go after that life you always imagined, the things you always desired. Go after what you want with all of your mind and soul.

Ask yourself the following questions to eradicate mental stumps and to discover your purpose:

1. Do you have any mental stumps in your life? If so, think of ways you will overcome them.
2. Have you determined the meaning of your life? Do you feel like you're moving in that direction? If not, why not?

3. What have been your expectations for your life? Have they been too low? If so, what can you do to increase your expectations for your life now?

4. List three major areas of your life that you need to snap out of the complacency coma. What impact would it have if you don't wake up?

5. What are five things you have to end in your life in order to create your new beginning?

CHAPTER 9

You Can Be Happy

For a happy life is joy in the truth.

– Augustine

Re-Discovering Happiness

Once upon a time, a community of eagles lived on a beautiful mountain range. They were carefree and happy and found an abundance of natural foods in the surrounding woods and streams. Their days were spent flying high above everything with peaceful pleasure.

Down on the dry grasslands below, there were a bunch of clever crows. They were merchants by trade and had invested their money in growing a low grade of corn. Looking around for potential customers, they spotted the high-flying eagles and plotted on ways to get them to come down to them.

"We will wrap the corn in fancy glittering packages that sparkle," said one crow. "When this catches their attention, they'll come down, and it will be easy for us to sell them the corn. Then we'll convince them that they must have our corn because without it they'll be lonely, loveless, lost, and will live in fear. When we make them feel guilty for ignoring our corn even though we know it's not the best, we've got them."

The eagles were intelligent but somewhat careless in their thinking. They saw the corn and it looked pretty good. It would definitely save them the effort of going to look for food on their own. So the eagles soared less and less and dropped down to the cornfields more and more. The less they flew, the less they felt like flying, and they eventually became comfortable going down to get the low-grade corn. They were no longer using their wings, so they became weak and had to hop around on the ground. This led to a lot of collisions with one another, followed by a lot of fighting, arguing, and distrust.

There was one eagle that sensed something was wrong about the whole operation. Besides, the corn just didn't taste right. When he tried to convince his friends to return to the mountains, the crows ridiculed him and called him a troublemaker. Believing the crows, the other eagles turned on their friend.

So the more corn the crows sold, the more the eagles became dependent. The once lofty kings of birds began to complain a lot, and they became nervous and irritable. They felt unhappy, lonely, loveless and lost. Every once in a while, they would remember their mountain home and their ability to soar, but they couldn't remember the way back. Other times, they knew something wasn't right, but figured this was the way life was supposed to go. And so they sullenly existed, hoping for something better to turn up, but it never did.

Growing tired, frustrated and confused with all of this, the keen-eyed eagle started doing something. He no longer waited for things to change. He stopped complaining and fighting his conditions and started to study himself very carefully. In rediscovering himself, he realized the wings that he once took for granted could be good for flying, so he decided to give them another try. They worked. So off he flew back to the mountain. He broke free from the things that he once thought held him hostage and realized he could fly above it all the moment he decided to take flight. From morning to sunset, he soared over his world, carefree and happy.

Many of us are like these eagles. We're caught up by the glitz and glamor of what we've been sold on about who, what or how we should be. We come to desire a certain type of lifestyle, career, home, or person to be with. Once we are sold on it, we realize it's cheap quality and not want we wanted. It doesn't make us happy. We begin doing things that are simply not fun anymore. The things that looked shiny and full of glitz in the beginning have no substance. Even though we know things aren't right, we keep hanging with the crows. We've become comfortable with them, and it's painful to leave because the crows have us believing a lie. Only when we become tired of our frustration and unhappiness can we destroy what's kept us back so we can fly up and away to our natural freedom and happiness, just as the eagles did. We have to know that happiness is not something to be pursued. It is something we must become by discovering who we are and what we can do.

Happiness is a State of Mind

Buddha tells of a traveler who is passing through the forest when he's seen and pursued by a tiger. The traveler runs frantically until he gets to a cliff. Once there, he notices a vine hanging down, so he uses it to lower himself down over the side of the cliff. However, the vine is too short for him to reach the ground, and he's left hanging far above the ground. Then he spots another tiger below growling viciously. So he has a tiger above him and one below him. Nothing could be worse. As he's hanging there, the traveler sees a juicy strawberry growing on the side of the cliff. He extends his arm, grabs it, bites into it, and says, "How delicious!" totally forgetting he's trapped between two tigers with nowhere to go.

Many of us settle for temporary satisfaction that ultimately leaves us unfilled because we don't understand that happiness is a state of mind that we can experience whenever we wish by changing our thinking. The traveler in Buddha's story was able to achieve happiness even though he appeared to be trapped and in danger when he refocused his thoughts. The thoughts that occupy our minds each and every day of our lives either produce feelings of happiness, despair, or they fall somewhere in between. Describing your problems won't heal them. Pointing out places where you do not measure up will never improve you. Self-depreciation is a vicious misuse of your mind. Stop telling others the story of your unhappiness and stop holding yourself hostage. Start to praise yourself and the good things about you. Start looking for good things in all that you do. When you praise yourself and appreciate who you are, you'll want to move forward in life. Your spoken words have power. Use them to produce the happiness that you want and not the unhappiness that you don't. Tell yourself that regardless of what is going on, you do not want unhappiness anymore, and your relationship with it is terminated.

How to Be Happy

To be happy, set up a daily routine of thoughts, feelings, and actions that produce happiness. Life has equipped us with intelligence and emotion. It offers every opportunity in the world to select what we want, including our happiness. Once you decide what you want with determination, everything moves into action through you. This is the action that knows no defeat. Regardless of what is going on around you, you can choose to be happy. You must come to the realization that happiness is a lifestyle. You can create it by questions like "What kind of life would I really want to live?" and "What would I look forward to waking up every morning and doing?"

When you are determined to be happy, your actions will do all the speaking for you. Most people spend their entire lives talking about happiness as if it's some place they'll magically stumble upon. They wish to get to it but don't realize the happiness starts with them right where they are. Happiness comes when you're true to yourself and understand that the meaning of happiness is different for each person. Happiness is yours for the taking, but it requires your willingness to finally let go of whatever you are unhappy with presently and launch out into the path of your dreams.

To do this, you need a routine. You can create a routine that produces happiness by choosing to think about what you wish to think about, what you wish to do, and the things you want to be. Focusing on these things and taking action to create them will ultimately bring about the happiness you desire. You have to surround yourself with the joys of life. Yes, there may be some challenges that come in the form of environment, unfinished school, struggling as a single parent, the loss of employment, or perhaps you made some really awful mistakes in the past that you're not happy about. Don't allow focusing on these things to sidetrack you from what you want in your life, the goals you want to achieve, and the happiness you seek.

Don't Put Your Happiness Off Until Tomorrow

P. D. Ouspensky once wrote about a man who finds life to be so intolerable that he decides to visit a magician.

"If I can just go back over my life to the younger years and start again, I would do things so much differently," he thinks.

The magician assures the man that going back in time wouldn't make much of a difference because he'd only repeat the same mistakes. The man is completely shocked by the magician's answer, so he asks to be sent back to his youth to find out if it's true. The magician agrees and sends the man back twelve years.

To his surprise, the man goes through the very same disappointing experiences in the exact same manner. Every tragic thing happened the same way again. He is amazed to find out that even though he had good intentions, he had no power to alter the course of his life.

When the man returned to the magician in disbelief and asked why things occurred in his life the way they did, the magician explained that for events to be different, the man must be different. His inward nature must be transformed and made new. This newness means persistent work on oneself, which will set new causes into motion. It's only at that point when things become different.

Thomas Carlyle once said that a human being can be compared to a ship without a rudder. If the wind blows one way, that's where they'll go, and if the wind blows another way, they go in that direction. If landfall should appear, which is their destination, they would have no clue that's where they are going. Many people constantly look backwards, wishing to go back and make the decisions they could have made to change the negative results they're dealing with today. In the interim, they're being tossed by this issue and by that issue and continue to soak in their unhappiness like they're sitting in a warm bath, planning for a day of happiness like it's some special holiday.

You shouldn't put your happiness off until tomorrow for two reasons. The first reason is tomorrow won't bend, move, or adjust to our demands. The second is that when we think of something that will make us happy tomorrow, we only postpone the enjoyment we could have today. It is usually not until we get to a place in life where we throw up our hands and say, "I can't do this anymore" that we are willing to make changes and stop putting off our happiness.

You Don't Have to Be Bored with Life

I'm often shocked by how many people say they're bored. I think about all the possibilities in life and wonder how in the world anyone could be bored, because there's just so much to do, see, and learn. Boredom is a negative mental and emotional state that breeds unhappiness. If in it too long, boredom can become destructive, because it causes us to look at past accomplishments and milestones instead of focusing on today. Boredom is one of the greatest causes of being unhappy. It's simply feeling like there is nothing left to do, like we have conquered all.

Isaac Newton once said, "What we know is a drop, what we don't know is the ocean," meaning there is so much more to life, there is so much more to do, there is so much more to have, and so much more to be than what we've experienced. We have to take advantage of the opportunities, inventions, and ideas at our disposal to break out of boredom. When we have people to meet and goals to achieve, boredom will have no place in our lives.

Perhaps we have gotten a bit too comfortable with how far the world is advancing. Since we have so much to do, we don't know what to do first or at all. Some of us are unfulfilled and don't know what to do because the things that we have to do aren't any fun, so we do things to take our minds off of our reality. This keeps us trapped on an endless roller coaster that takes us up and down but never brings us true happiness. I want you to ask yourself: am I bored with the things I am doing currently? Is life boring to me because I've repeated the same things for years? Am I tired of trying to do and be something I'm not? Is life fun for me anymore?

If you are bored and life is no longer enjoyable, it's important that you go to work quickly to break up the boredom mindset immediately.

True Happiness

Many of us go from birth to death experiencing only a few moments of true happiness. Happiness seems evasive. One second we have it, the next it's gone. True happiness is genuine satisfaction with your present experience regardless of what is going on. When I say satisfaction, what I mean is a deep underlying sense of fulfillment. A sense of doing a good job with life. Satisfaction comes from knowing who you are and having the ability to create the world that you want on the inside and ultimately make that world your reality. The happiness we search for is within our reach. We have the ability to think ourselves into our own happiness. No one can keep us from happiness except ourselves. Think about some of the things you can be happy about. If you don't know where to start, think about the simple fact that you have an opportunity, by being alive today, to create the world you want to live in.

Take a look at where you are in your life and think of the five closest people to you. How many of them are truly satisfied with their current situations? Unhappy people always think they know why they are unhappy and can give a lengthy list of all the reasons why, but most of it is incorrect. The truth is they're unhappy because they just simply don't see themselves correctly. They want to change the circumstances, events, people and other things in their lives, but they don't believe they themselves need to change. They want to rearrange the effects they're getting by dodging the cause. A change in awareness is the answer.

Raymond C. Barker once said, "The principle of life is that life responds by corresponding. Your life becomes the thing or things you have decided it shall be."

We must take accountability and stop making excuses. Life becomes to you what you are to it. Happiness is not based on happenings, although that can bring you temporary happiness.

Don't Feed the Animals

I remember going to the zoo and reading the No Feeding the Animals sign. I found it interesting, because while we may have a kind heart toward animals and wish to help them by giving them food, our giving can cause a few issues. One problem with feeding the animals is that they will bring more animals to you if you feed them. The second is that animals can become violent when food is offered to them.

Negative feelings that fuel unhappiness are like animals that attack when we feed them. If there's an attack on your emotions, it's important that you see the attack for what it is and no longer feed it with emotional energy. When you define what's attacking you, you'll know the best way to move forward. We must understand all attacks are the same, they just come from different places, people or things. If you don't, what you experience in life will immediately become negative and evil, and it will become destructive to your forward progress.

We must see that our negative emotions are self-induced suffering. Can we be happy and mad at the same time? No. Can we be depressed and enjoy ourselves? No. Can you live in a constant state of worry and enjoy your day? It's pretty tough. Negative emotions have a subtle way of slipping in through the back door, and before you know it, you're submerged in unhappiness because you kept feeding the emotions and they grew. To combat this, you have to keep your feelings and thoughts out of it and develop a clear perception of what's happening at the moment it begins. There is no enemy that has any power to hurt you when you're aware of the power that lies within you. Don't feed the animals; they only become bigger obstacles to overcome. Feed the good that you want in your life and focus on your happiness.

Ask yourself the following questions to evaluate your beliefs about obtaining happiness:

1. Do you believe that you can be happy?
2. If you're unhappy, are you willing to change your thoughts about your situation to produce a better outcome?
3. Do you postpone your happiness for other people, places, and things?
4. How often do you find yourself saying, "I'll be happy as soon as...?"
5. Do you find yourself feeding the animals?

CHAPTER 10

Wake Up & Win

The whole course of things goes to teach us faith.
We need only obey.

– Ralph Waldo Emerson

No Retreating

There once was a great war general who faced a tough set of circumstances. The situation was tough because it not only affected him but also his army. A decision had to be made. He was going to send his army against a powerful enemy that greatly outnumbered his own. He put all of his soldiers onto the boats he had and sailed into the enemy's territory. What he decided to do next was powerful. He ordered everyone to get off of the boats, unloaded all of the equipment, then gave the order to burn all of the ships.

He gathered his men and said, "You see, we don't have a way out. The way we came is not the way we're going to leave. The only way we can leave is if we win. We don't have any other option. We win or we die."

They won.

When you're ready to finally take charge of your life and get off the sidelines, you have to wake up, get up, and get on the battlefield to win. There is opportunity all around you, but you have to develop a desire to be, do, and have what you want. You will be ready to receive the things you desire when retreating is no longer an option, and you wake up to the idea that you can win. Wishing for prosperity, happiness, health, or any other good thing will never bring it into manifestation. The only way you can bring the things you want into reality is by turning them into an obsession then planning definite and concrete ways to get them. This must be followed by persistence that does not understand retreat. You will never be ready to have something until you believe you can really have it, and you put in the work. The only way to strengthen your belief is by spending time seeing yourself in the possession of the goals, ideas, and dreams you think about. This has to be done over and over again. The greatest of achievements started as a dream. That dream was so strong, so powerful, so inspiring that it became something that the person who achieved it was willing to burn all of their boats to get to. In other words, there was no turning back.

What will it take for you to finally wake up? What needs to happen in your life for you to be ready to win? What will it take for you to finally be tired of being defeated by things you know you can beat? Do you know that you're never defeated until you accept the idea that you are? Do you know that you will never be a winner until you accept the idea that you are? If what you want to do in life is right and just, and you believe deep down inside that it's for you, then make a move and go for it. Go all out, give it your all, and don't worry about what anyone may say, think, or do. Never mind if you are hit with temporary setbacks. For you to win, you have to develop a winning mindset, a winning awareness. You have to think of the ideas and goals in the present that you wish to have in the future. When you do this daily, you will automatically remove all that is not in line with what you desire. It will also automatically produce a snowball effect.

Emerson once said, "The whole course of things goes to teach us faith. We need only obey." If we keep retreating and worrying about how things will turn out, we will never truly know what faith is or learn the lesson that the process of following our dreams can teach us.

Remove the Obstruction

During a recent meeting, one of my clients told me that one of her biggest challenges is believing that she can actually achieve what she really wants to. She created her image, made a plan, and looked at her vision every day, but for some reason she was stuck because she kept having thoughts that told her that what she wanted was too large for her to actually accomplish.

She said, "Jermain, I have a wall up. Every time I go to do what I know I should, I get blocked by that wall and find myself doing nothing."

In listening to her, I realized that she truly believed that the wall was the reason she was not getting to her goals. So I asked her what kind of wall she was looking at? Was it the Great Wall of China, or was it the size of the wall we were sitting next to in my office? I wanted to know the size of what was in her way.

She sat there and thought for a few moments, but she really couldn't tell me what type of wall it was. In actuality, she was creating the obstruction. The image of a wall caused her to believe that what she wanted to do was so big that it just didn't make any sense to accomplish it, that what she wanted was too complicated.

I told her that in order for her to win, she had to deny that the obstruction existed and move forward with the belief that she could achieve her goals, no matter what. She had to burn her boats, so that staying stuck or retreating was no longer an option.

You Can Win

Have you ever thought about something that you wanted to accomplish more than once per day? Has it ever woken you up in the middle of the night?

Winston Churchill once said, "Never give up on something that you can't go a whole day thinking about." In other words, don't stop climbing.

As a mountain climber climbs to the top of a mountain, there are two things he must do. First, he never stops thinking about where he wants to be. Second, he lets go of where he is so he can reach a higher point that will allow him to pull himself closer to his destination. As tough as it may be, if he never lets go of the level he's on and only pays attention to where he is, he'll lose ground. Just hanging on is not the goal. The higher goal, the thing he truly wants to get to, is the mountain top. He has to stretch and reach for it. He has to constantly think about it. He has to let go to grow.

Many of us can't get to our next level simply because we stopped reaching for what we wanted. We let go of our dreams instead of letting go of the things that stopped us from climbing, and then spent years holding on to them in resentment. We have been hanging on to places, people, and things, not realizing they are causing us a huge delay in getting us to where we really want to be.

Every day, we should reach, stretch, and grow to get to our dream even when it hurts. Even when we don't want to, we have to press on. Think about your last few years and ask yourself what you have been reaching and climbing toward. Have you been climbing the right mountain or even climbing a mountain at all? If you haven't been, I encourage you to put on your mountain climbing gear and make up in your mind that today is the day you're going to begin to climb the mountain of your dreams. Once you find the mountaintop, you'll realize that it was not some legend. It's real and it's yours.

Can you win? That's a question that only you can answer. All things are already working for your good. Now it's time for you to step forward and stop sitting around waiting for what you want to happen. You may have some mental blocks regarding success, even though you did not choose to have them. They may be there because you unconsciously allowed the news, media, family, your environment, or the opinions of others to come in and tell you an untruth. Any person with courage and belief in themselves who knows what they want can change their lives from failure to success. We are not only born with the ability to succeed, but we also have the drive deep down for it.

Can you win? The answer is yes. But do you want to? Our minds have a tendency to use all sorts of reasons why we can't succeed. When you want to win, you'll see right through these false reasons. The person who is a failure has used a process, and the successful person has used the same process. That means there's one process, and you direct it. You win or you don't. Whatever you decide must appear. Life says that you can become what you choose, but only when you choose it and are willing to go through the necessary change.

Today I want you to assume a winning attitude. Accept success as true for you and watch it begin to happen. Select something you want to accomplish and get it done. It's important for you to set a goal that you can accomplish immediately, because it starts the habit of victory. And any victory, whether large or small, creates a winning mindset. One of the main reasons we don't win consistently is because we have too many gaps between victories, and in those gaps, we have too many negative ideas, resentments, failures, and worries. The way to overcome that is to set targets that you are consistently reaching toward. This is how you develop the idea that you can win. Take one step toward your goal immediately, then another step and another step, and in the process, you'll form a pattern of accomplishment.

What we must understand is that we also win in the process of getting to our goals, because every step is a win. When we finally reach our goal, we prove to ourselves that we have the ability to do what we desire. Worry, fear, and negative circumstances, while they will appear, will no longer hold us hostage when we live a life that serves as our purpose and we move steadily toward what we desire. That way, winning becomes a wonderful game to play.

Something New

Once in a while, we get a glimpse of something new, a better life for ourselves. We peek at it temporarily only to revert to our norm because we don't believe that we can have it. No one is happy twenty-four hours a day, but too many of us are happy too few hours each day. That stems in part from the idea that we can't have the good things we truly want.

Despite all of this, we seem to always want something new, anything that can help us get to the happiness we seek. The fact is when you have true satisfaction, you'll no longer look outside of yourself for it, and you'll live more easily. In order to have something new, you must do something new, something different. For this to happen, your mindset has to stay on the level of solution rather than the level of problem. This is where we move from fight, worry, and fear to controlled attention on the things we want, followed solely by appropriate action. This is the way life was truly meant for us to live.

Today, I want you to look in the mirror and promise that you'll stop complaining about whatever is going on in your life right now that you disagree with. Have you ever noticed how critical a person who is not winning is? They constantly talk down about everything. When you follow a pattern like this, winning is suppressed and negative results typically follow. Drop what you have been carrying. If you cannot physically do anything about it, accept that there is nothing you can do. Stop telling others about what you are dealing with. Leave it in the past. Start instead looking for the good things in life. Find positive things to talk about and to work toward. Start looking for good things in all that you do, everywhere that you are, and in the people you're around. Watch your conversations, and focus on the positive. Your words do have power. Use them to produce what you want and not what you don't. Start doing things in a new way. Start eating differently. Start waking up early. Start being more excited about the new life that you are creating for yourself. We want something to happen first before change, but the way to get something new in your life is to do something first, and then the new thing you want will come.

As Ralph Waldo Emerson once said, "Do the thing and you will have the power."

Program to Win

Your life is all that you have. Every day that goes by is a priceless possession. The world will continue to move on whether you win or not. You can live life winning, or you can live life losing. To think that success can happen without inner change is like assuming you can think negative thoughts and expect good things to happen. They won't. The true path to success is narrow and straight, yet many people believe there's no path at all, or they can hop on and off at convenient times. That's far from the truth. It's our success program that leads us to a winning life.

If we want to play sports or an instrument and become great at it, we work on it until we're confident. The confidence in our ability to do well comes from the specific path we took to master what we wanted to learn, which programmed us with the knowledge necessary to succeed. There's no difference in the results we want in life. The principles don't change. In order to get the winning results you want, you have to program yourself to win. It's important to maintain a positive mental attitude no matter what happens in the process. Programming yourself means to see yourself doing, being, and having the things you want. It also requires you to build a winning image. If you are going to get results, you'll need to have confidence in yourself. Gaining confidence requires you to speak positively to yourself daily and to cancel all negative ideas about yourself. It requires you to read and listen to things that motivate and encourage you to be the best, to be laser-focused on your goals, and to constantly see yourself as a person who accomplishes things by taking action.

There are only three reasons why we won't program ourselves for success:

1. Our thinking needs to be reprogrammed.
2. We have not found the right path.
3. We think that once we win in one area, there's nothing else to win at.

To overcome these difficulties, program your mind to where you want to be. If you have not found the right path to win yet, keep working, keep searching, and keep looking for ideas. Far too often, we get caught up in focusing on things not working as opposed to finding a way to make them work.

Your capacity to become something new is not dependent on what you have been; it is dependent on what you are—and you can improve that through your programming. In every one of us there is something that says, "I know I can be better than I am."

You can always become better. When you change your belief about you, your experiences change. If you don't like where you are or what you are, a change in belief will cause your circumstances to change.

Life has held you hostage and kept you from moving forward, but it hasn't destroyed you, because there's something deep down inside of you that wants to wake up and win. There is something in you that worry can never destroy but that your faith and your vision can affirm and use to make you the person you need to be. You are going to be greater than what you were, stronger than what has happened, and you can speed up the process as you realize that deep within you, there is something that makes you greater than where you are at the moment.

You need only to Wake up and Win.

Affirmations:

- The Power within me is greater than any obstacle before me.
- Failure is a thing of the past. Winning is the reality of my present and my future.
- The winning purpose of my soul vibrates through my thoughts each and every day.
- I contain universal perfection. I am a winner.

Made in USA - North Chelmsford, MA
1042572_9781708665784
01.08.2020 1151